Kindergarten P.E.T.S.™

By
Sandy Wyatt
Dodie Merritt

CLC0412
© 2007 Pieces of Learning
Marion IL
ISBN 978-1-934358-00-9
www.piecesoflearning.com
Cover by John Steele
Printed by Royal Palm Press
U.S.A.

08/2017

Table of Contents

Acknowledgments

The authors of this book would like to thank:

- *the administration of IL Prairie Hill School District #133 for their inspiration and support of this K-PETS™ program;*
- *Shannon Anderson, in whose Kindergarten classes these materials were field-tested; and*
- *the IL Crystal Lake and Genoa-Kingston School Districts #47 and #424 for launching the original PETS™ programs.*

Special thanks to Elyse Wyatt
for the original artwork created for convergent and visual small group activities

and to our families for their on-going patience and support

K-PETS™

(Kindergarten Primary Education Thinking Skills)

WHAT <u>IS</u> K-PETS™?

PETS™ is a systematized enrichment and diagnostic thinking skills program that can be easily integrated into an existing primary curriculum. PETS™ serves the dual purpose of helping in the identification of academically talented students as well as teaching <u>all</u> students higher-level thinking skills. K- PETS™ is a Kindergarten curriculum that introduces students to different ways of thinking. While intended to set the stage for the PETS™123 series, K- PETS™ can definitely be used on its own.

IS K-PETS™ GOOD FOR <u>ALL</u> STUDENTS?

Yes! First of all, K-PETS™ is aligned with the taxonomy of Benjamin Bloom, presenting lessons in convergent analysis, divergent synthesis, and critical evaluation. These higher-level thinking skills are often less emphasized in most primary curricula, yet students of <u>all</u> ability levels have shown interest in and understanding of these different types of thinking. More importantly, <u>these</u> are the problem-solving strategies that are critical for all children to know and feel comfortable using throughout their lives.

Through lessons that specifically target one thinking strategy, students with strengths in that particular area have the opportunity to be recognized. In an educational environment that tends to be convergent in nature, lessons in creative divergent and visual thinking can be critical for students who may be less academically successful. When these other strengths are recognized and validated, self-esteem soars.

Secondly, K- PETS™ activities correlate with the multiple intelligences as defined by Howard Gardner. Recognizing that there is a diversity of ways in which children internalize information, the K- PETS™ lessons engage children through a mixture of approaches.

HOW DOES K-PETS™ WORK AS AN IDENTIFICATION TOOL?

The PETS™ series also provides teachers with the opportunity to build behavioral portfolios on students that will help in identifying cognitively talented students early in their school careers in order to implement a curriculum that will best suit their special needs. This identification occurs in the classroom setting during whole class and small group lessons. Specific behaviors are monitored and logged on behavioral checklists.

WHAT'S THE DELIVERY SYSTEM FOR K-PETS™?

The format of the K-PETS™ delivery system follows a modification of the Enrichment Triad Model posed by Dr. Joseph Renzulli. Initially, the entire class experiences the challenge of each new thinking skill through two whole class lessons which last 30 minutes each per week of instruction. Subsequently, <u>all</u> Kindergarten students participate in the follow-up small group activities. Groups of four to six students are pulled out until <u>every</u> child has participated in the 30-minute pull-out session for each thinking skill. These groups can meet in a different area or at a back table within the classroom.

However, as this curriculum is designed to be very flexible in order to meet the needs of students and for scheduling purposes, feel free to combine the two whole class lessons into one 40-minute session. As the different activities are varied in content and approach, children tend not to lose attentiveness. Conversely, doing more, shorter sessions is perfectly acceptable, too. Supplementing each unit with more activities that effectively reinforce concepts is also highly recommended.

When identification as well as enrichment is a goal of the program, a specialist delivers the whole class lessons while the classroom teacher logs student behaviors on the observation checklists. During the small group sessions, the specialist manages both lesson delivery and the behavioral checklist in order to further evaluate student potential for appropriate student programming.

If identification of academically talented students is not an issue, a classroom teacher can easily implement K- PETS™ as an enrichment program for students. Small group activities can be additional whole class lessons while others will adapt well into learning center activities.

CAN OTHER MATERIALS BE ADDED TO THE K-PETS™ PROGRAM?

Absolutely. There is a list of suggested extension resources at the end of each of the four units in the *Resources & Extensions* sections. These resources include many more trade books as well as games and other manipulatives that can be used to reinforce the thinking strategies introduced in each unit. <u>**NOTE**</u>: *Good sources for any of these great books that may now be out-of-print are the second-hand booksellers on Amazon.com.*

There are also generic sets of questions in each *Resources & Extensions* section to use with any additional resources designed to reinforce the thinking strategies presented in the whole group lessons. The questions are on separate strips. Copy each type of question in a different color and then cut them apart for flexibility of use. Choose a specific, desired set of questions or pull questions at random from a cup.

Put a different question on each side of a cube for another variation (see the PETS™ Q'ubes™ in each *Resources & Extensions* section). Tell the students to roll the cube and answer the question that appears on top. This is a particularly appealing hands-on, kinesthetic approach for young learners.

PROGRAM OVERVIEW

PETS™ has a two-tier delivery system which is easily facilitated by the classroom teacher or visiting specialist. At all levels, the first tier focuses on whole class enrichment activities for the entire grade level population that engage students in higher-level convergent, divergent, evaluative, and visual thinking. In K-PETS™, the second tier activities are used in small group settings with <u>all</u> students. However, in PETS™ levels 1, 2, and 3, these second tier activities are used in the small group settings to challenge only the more capable students.

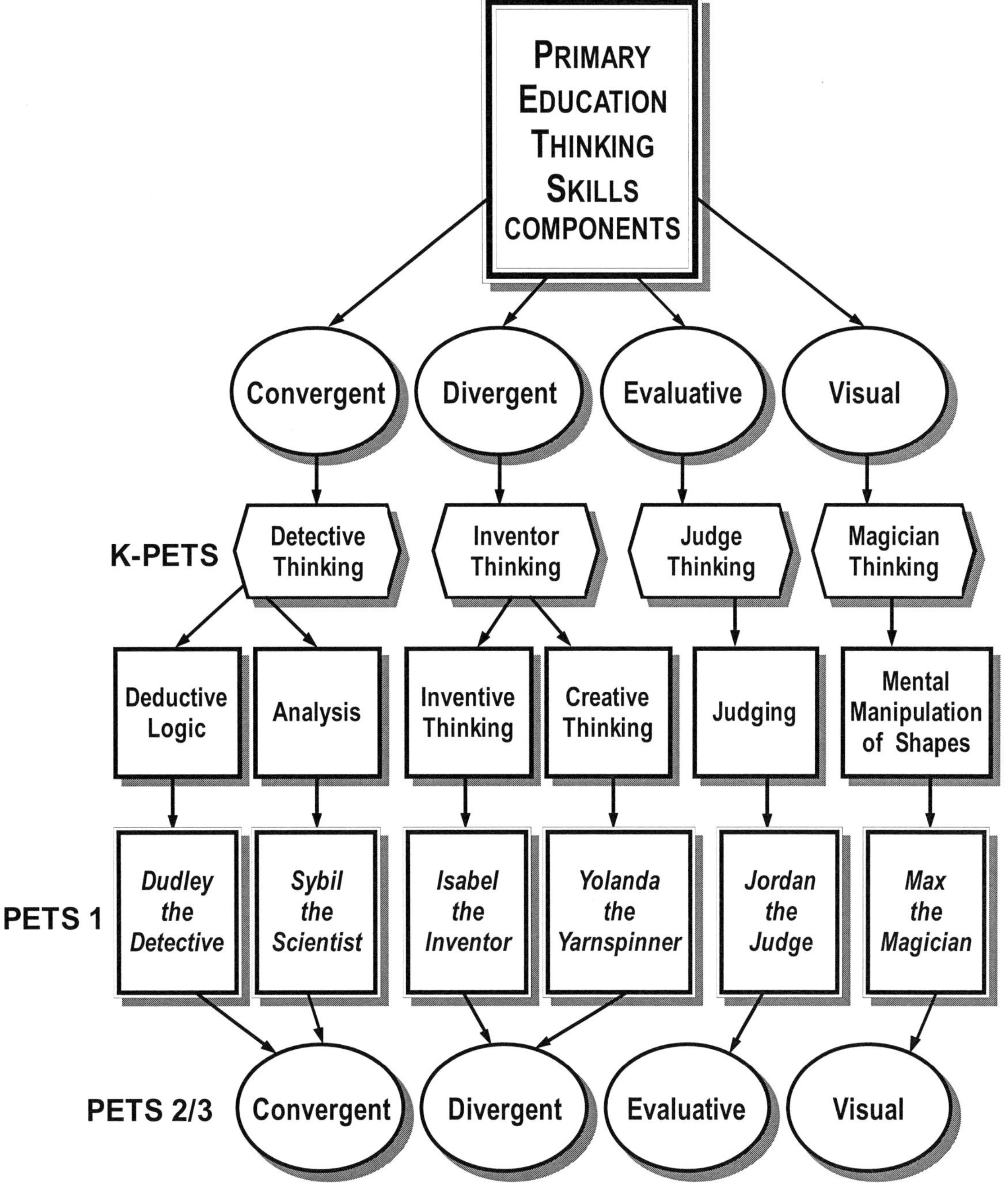

K-PETS™ & Bloom's Taxonomy

	Convergent	Divergent	Visual	Evaluative
Evaluation *Judge it!*				X
Synthesis *Change it!*		X	X	X
Analysis *Examine it!*	X	X	X	X
Application *Use it!*	X	X	X	X
Comprehension *Explain it!*	X	X	X	X
Knowledge *Name it!*	X	X	X	X

K-PETS™ Whole Class Lessons & Multiple Intelligences

	Convergent	Divergent	Visual	Evaluative
Verbal/Linguistic *Word smart*	X	X	X	X
Logical/Mathematical *Logic smart*	X	X	X	X
Visual/Spatial *Picture smart*	X	X	X	X
Musical/Rhythmic *Music smart*	X	X		
Bodily/Kinesthetic *Body smart*	X	X		X
Intrapersonal *Self smart*	X		X	X
Interpersonal *People smart*	X	X	X	X
Naturalist *Nature smart*	X			

K-PETS™ Small Group Lessons & Multiple Intelligences

	Convergent	Divergent	Visual	Evaluative
Verbal/Linguistic *Word smart*	X	X	X	X
Logical/Mathematical *Logic smart*	X	X	X	X
Visual/Spatial *Picture smart*	X	X	X	X
Musical/Rhythmic *Music smart*				
Bodily/Kinesthetic *Body smart*	X	X		X
Intrapersonal *Self smart*	X	X	X	X
Interpersonal* *People smart*				
Naturalist *Nature smart*	X			

* As most small group lessons are designed to identify individual students who fully understand that thinking strategy and to encourage individual work and ideas, not shared ideas, the Interpersonal Intelligence is generally not a focus during these sessions.

IDENTIFYING TALENTED LEARNERS

The Kindergarten classroom teacher has a very diverse population in both maturity and intellect. Some students will immediately appear talented in certain areas, while other students will need to be given opportunities to show their abilities. Before attempting to use the behavioral observation checklists, teachers need to understand the different characteristics and behaviors which indicate that a student may be talented in a particular area.

CONVERGENT/ANALYTICAL THINKING

During each lesson, look for students who demonstrate logical reasoning by identifying and using clues to determine the correct solution to a problem. They tend to see the interrelationships between clues and defer judgment until all clues have been collected. Many times they will display outside knowledge about a topic that will help them discover the solution. The ability to see intuitively the correct answer is another characteristic of students who excel at deductive/convergent thinking. Students who display much enthusiasm during the activity should be observed carefully as well.

DIVERGENT/CREATIVE THINKING

During each lesson, look for students who can list many responses to questions or brainstorm many ideas. Not only are they fluent in their thinking, but they are also very flexible. They may have many unusual, off-beat, and creative ideas that are sometimes very humorous. These students can elaborate on their own ideas or ideas of others, often displaying an advanced vocabulary. Students who display much enthusiasm during the activity should be observed carefully as well.

VISUAL/SPATIAL THINKING

During the whole class lesson, look for students who are able to manipulate shapes mentally in order to achieve a solution. These students have good memories for visual details. They often enjoy activities involving hands-on building of three-dimensional objects. Since these students may not be as verbal as their classmates, they may not have as much opportunity to demonstrate their talents during traditional classroom activities. They often respond best to visual images such as graphic organizers and instructional computer programs. Students who display much enthusiasm during the activity should be observed carefully as well.

EVALUATIVE/CRITICAL THINKING

During the whole class lesson, look for students who are able to make choices and offer solutions that are based on factual, measurable, or observable considerations. These students recognize more than one viewpoint and understand how different considerations, or criteria, can affect outcome. They can support their decisions and opinions. Students who display much enthusiasm during the activity should be observed carefully as well.

                                                         © **Pieces of Learning**

IDENTIFYING TALENTED LEARNERS DURING WHOLE CLASS LESSONS

The K-PETS™ program can help both classroom and specialty teachers identify talented students in whole class situations and small group situations. The whole class lessons are the first tier in identifying students. The ideal situation is to have two teachers in the classroom, one teacher/specialist presenting the thinking skill lesson and the classroom teacher observing student behaviors. If two teachers are not available, the program will work with a teacher's aide. If this is the case, the teacher can help the aide by using key phrases to indicate when and where a tally mark should be added on the teacher observation checklist. For example, a teacher may say, *"Wow, Julie, that's a great way to use an earlier clue to see the new clue."*

A Teacher Observation Checklist is provided with each of the four units, one for each different thinking skill. There are six behavioral characteristics on each checklist that are considered to be indicators of potential talent for that type of thinking. These behaviors vary from thinking skill to thinking skill. The names of all the students in a class are listed on each checklist before starting each unit.

When a student is observed showing one of the identified behaviors, the teacher places a tally mark in the cell for that behavior following the student's name. If there are additional instances when the student demonstrates this behavior, the teacher adds additional tally marks. To differentiate between sessions, teachers may record each lesson's responses in different colors. Some specialty teachers may prefer to collect the checklists after each class and then return them to the classroom teacher at the start of the next lesson.

It is important for the teacher observing the students to look beyond just the most vocal students who are the first to answer. All students need to be observed and questioned to give all students an opportunity to show their potential.

It is essential for the teacher to remember that the number of talented learners in any one classroom may be quite small. As the PETS™ series has been designed to identify this small population, do not expect the entire class to achieve mastery of every new concept. All students will benefit from exposure to these higher-level thinking experiences, but the actual number of students demonstrating mastery level may be quite small. That's OK.

IDENTIFYING TALENTED LEARNERS DURING SMALL GROUP LESSONS

The second tier of the identification process is the small group lessons. These are groups of four to six students who may meet outside the classroom or at a back table within the classroom. Consider breaking each class into as many small group sessions as scheduling allows since this will help avoid the "copying of others' ideas" syndrome. Student behaviors can be far more carefully monitored in the small group setting.

The small group lessons are designed to provide further enrichment and opportunities for teachers to observe additional behaviors that identify talented learners. The more time spent with each student means more diagnostic data gathered. These lessons are not as structured as the whole class lessons and provide students with more opportunities for interaction and cooperative problem solving. They are designed to be diagnostic as opposed to instructional.

Divergent/Creative Thinking

During each lesson, the teacher and observer are looking for students who can list many responses to questions or brainstorm many ideas. Not only are they fluent in their thinking but they are also very flexible. They may have many unusual, offbeat, and creative ideas that are sometimes very humorous. These students can elaborate on their own ideas or on the ideas of others, often displaying an advanced vocabulary. Students who display much enthusiasm during the activity should be observed carefully as well.

Diagnostic Notes

An observation checklist is provided. Use the same checklist for both the whole class and small group recording. This way all of the data is together on one sheet. The following is a short summary of what to look for in student behaviors:

OFFERS MANY IDEAS (FLUENCY) – All responses are acceptable. Look for students who provide many.

CHANGES CATEGORIES OF IDEAS (FLEXIBILITY) – Note students who are able to change their course of thinking here.

OFFERS OFFBEAT IDEAS (ORIGINALITY) – Record the students with many ideas that are very different. The ideas may be so wacky that they could not actually be implemented, but note the originality on the checklist.

ADDS DETAILS TO OTHER IDEAS (ELABORATION) – A student who spends a long time adding details displays this behavior. Record a student who piggybacks on the ideas of other students.

USES ADVANCED VOCABULARY – These are students who correctly use words that classmates do not know. They sound very adult in the way in which they express themselves.

DISPLAYS MATURE SENSE OF HUMOR – Many students have a mature sense of humor. The divergent thinking activities provide opportunities for students to display this sense of humor.

Kindergarten PETS -- Teacher Observation Checklist
DIVERGENT/CREATIVE THINKING

Teacher: School Year:

Student Names	Offers Many Ideas (Fluency)	Changes Categories of Ideas (Flexibility)	Offers Offbeat Ideas (Originality)	Adds Details to Other Ideas (Elaboration)	Uses Advanced Vocabulary	Displays Mature Sense of Humor	Teacher Observations	TOTALS

Divergent/Creative
Inventor Thinking
Whole Class
Lesson 1

Purpose

The purpose of this lesson is to introduce **Inventor Thinking (divergent/creative brainstorming),** which allows students to see extraordinary possibilities in ordinary, everyday items or situations. Divergent/creative thinking focuses on the following concepts:

- ❖ There are many correct responses/possibilities (**fluency**).

- ❖ Ideas may begin from a common "stem" but branch in different directions from there (**flexibility**).

- ❖ All ideas are welcomed, even those that seem silly at the time (**originality**).

- ❖ It is important to see things creatively which helps produce many possibilities in ordinary events, situations, and objects.

- ❖ It is encouraged to piggyback ideas on those from others (**elaboration**).

Materials

- ❖ One copy of the book <u>Ten Black Dots</u> by Donald Crews (classroom-sized books are best, if available)

- ❖ An overhead projector

- ❖ Several black dots (die-cuts or *Black Dots*)

- ❖ A set of overhead markers

- ❖ *Teacher Observation Checklist – Divergent/Creative Thinking*

Lesson Plan

1. Introduce the lesson by asking if students know what an *inventor* is. Brainstorm some possible inventors and their inventions. Try to include some female inventors. Discuss with students what they think are some of the most important inventions. Point out the difference between inventing something and discovering something. Students may try to suggest that Ben Franklin invented electricity. Franklin *discovered* electricity but did not *invent* it. A discovery is something that already exists. An invention is a new idea or creation thought up by someone. The inventor is the first person to conceive the idea. The inventor may not actually make the objects. Sometimes an inventor will hire someone else to make it.

2. Tell the students that today they will use brainstorming to imagine what objects could be described in the story that you will be reading.

3. It is important that Kindergarteners continue to change venues, so at this point ask them to move to a reading area in which to share the story. This way all students can also see the pictures clearly.

4. During the activity below, the classroom teacher will gather data on the *Teacher Observation Checklist – Divergent/Creative Thinking* provided with each student's name on it.

5. Begin to read <u>Ten Black Dots</u>. Once you read each page, ask students to give new ideas as to what can be made with each number of dots. For example,

   a. What new idea does someone have for making something new using one black dot?

   b. What new idea does someone have for making something new using two black dots <u>together</u>?

   c. Does anyone have any ideas for using five black dots <u>together</u>?

   d. Does anyone have any ideas for using ten black dots <u>together</u>?

The word <u>together</u> is an important word to stress throughout this activity. Encourage students to generate one idea using all dots together, rather than multiple ideas for individual dots.

This is also a perfect opportunity to stress that no one should make fun of anyone else. Some of the world's greatest achievements have developed from the zaniest of ideas.

Occasionally act out an object for which a child has an idea. For example, if a child gives the idea of a smiley face for two black dots, ask all of the students to demonstrate a smiley face. Then ask them to show you the difference between a frowny face and a smiley face.

6. Once the book has been completed, ask the students to return to their desks or tables. While returning to their desks, sing, "One Little, Two Little, Three Little Indians," substituting "dots" for "Indians" (see #8).

7. At this point, you will recall some of the ideas presented during the reading of the story by using the dots and the markers on the overhead projector to demonstrate how dots can be connected to make something new. Here are two sample ideas:

Example for 2 dots:
A Smiley Face

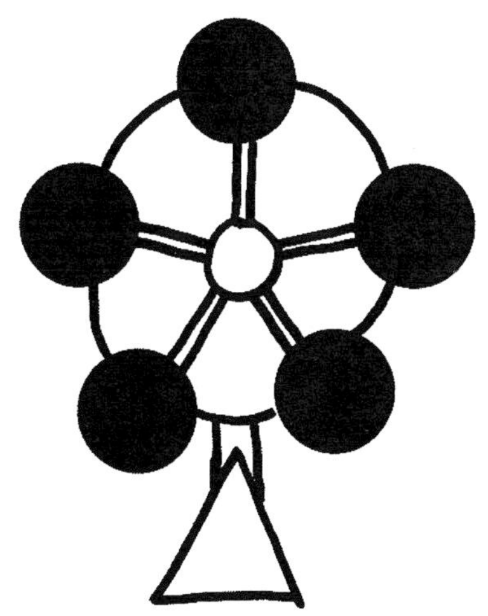

Example for 5 dots:
A Ferris Wheel

8. For closure to the lesson, sing the dot song again with all of the students:

>   One little, two little, three little dots,
>   Four little, five little, six little dots,
>   Seven little, eight little, nine little dots,
>   Ten little dots work for me.

Black Dots

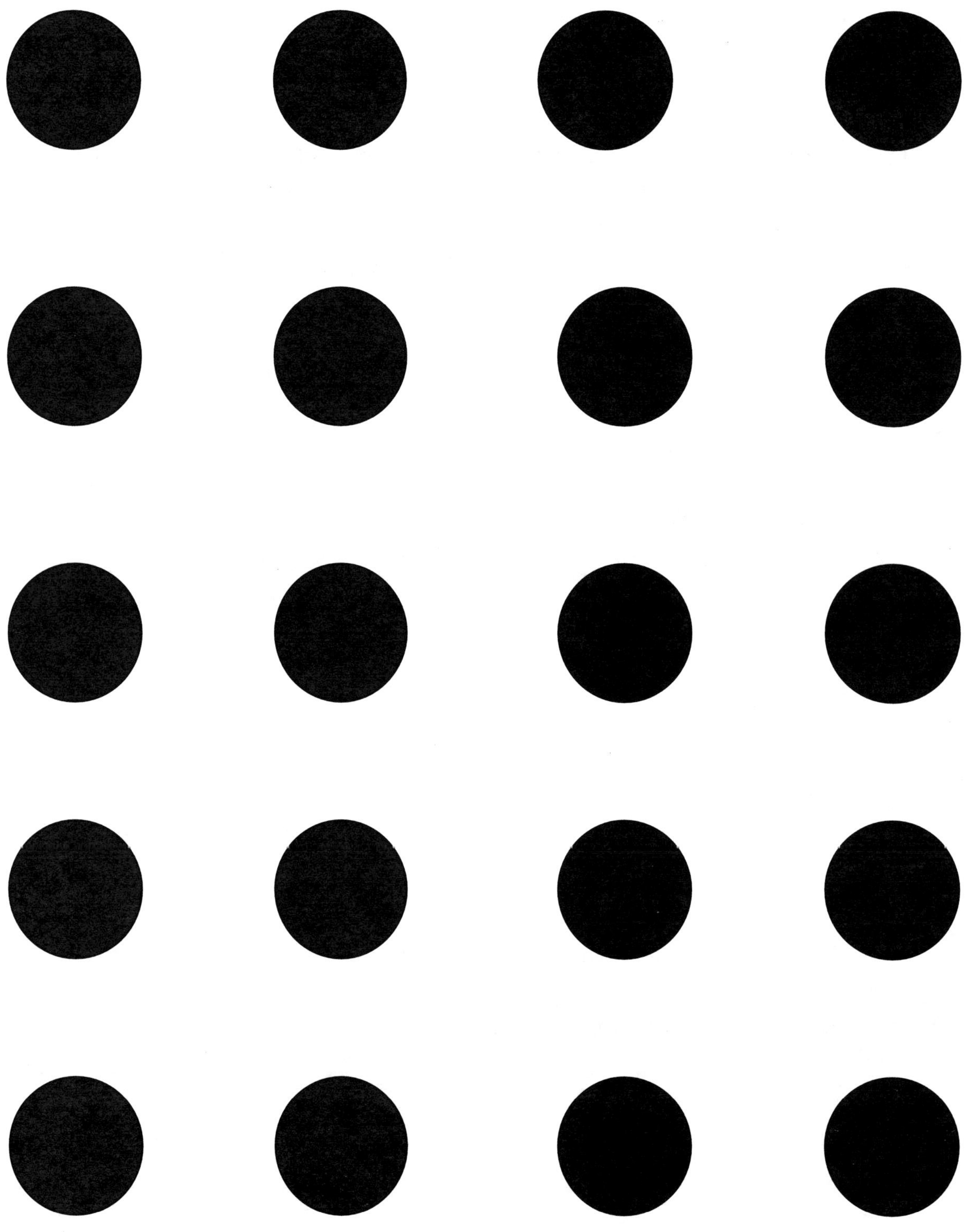

Divergent/Creative
Inventor Thinking
Whole Class
Lesson 2

Purpose

The purpose of this lesson is to reinforce **Inventor Thinking (divergent/creative brainstorming),** which allows students to see extraordinary possibilities in ordinary, everyday items or situations. Divergent/creative thinking focuses on the following concepts:

❖ There are many correct responses/possibilities (**fluency**).

❖ Ideas may begin from a common "stem" but branch in different directions from there (**flexibility**).

❖ All ideas are welcomed, even those that seem silly at the time (**originality**).

❖ It is important to see things creatively which helps produce many possibilities in ordinary events, situations, and objects.

❖ It is encouraged to piggyback ideas on those from others (**elaboration**).

Materials

❖ One copy of the book <u>Curious George's ABCs</u> by H.A. Rey (classroom-sized books are best, if available)

❖ An overhead projector

❖ Several black dots (die-cuts or *Black Dots*)

❖ Several black letters (die-cuts or *Alphabet*)

❖ A set of overhead markers

❖ *Teacher Observation Checklist – Divergent/Creative Thinking*

Lesson Plan

1. Introduce the lesson by reviewing what an *inventor* is. Have the class recall some of the inventors from the last session. Brainstorm other inventors and their inventions. Try to include some female inventors. Discuss with students what they think are some of the most important inventions. Again point out the difference between *inventing* something and *discovering* something. Review that a discovery is something that already exists. An invention is a new idea or creation thought up by someone. The inventor is the first person to conceive the idea. The inventor may not actually make the objects. Sometimes an inventor will hire someone else to make it.

2. Tell the students that today they will use brainstorming to imagine lots of new objects that could be added to the story that you will be reading.

3. It is important that Kindergarteners continue to change venues, so at this point you may wish to ask them to move to a reading area in which to share the story. This way all students can also see the pictures clearly.

4. During the activity below, the classroom teacher will gather data on the *Teacher Observation Checklist – Divergent/Creative Thinking* provided with each student's name on it.

5. Begin to read <u>Curious George's ABCs</u> by H.A. Rey. Once you read each page, ask students to give new ideas as to what can be made with each letter. (You may want to be selective and not take the time to do all 26 letters). For example:

    a. What new idea does someone have for making something new using an "A"? Could you use any black dots to complete your picture?

    b. What new idea does someone have for making something new using a "B" and some black dots <u>together</u>?

    c. Does anyone have any ideas for using an "O"? Could you use some black dots to complete that picture?

    d. Does anyone have any ideas for using a "Q" and two black dots <u>together</u>?

    e. Stand up and show me what an "S" looks like.

    f. Stand up and show me what a "W" looks like. Can anyone demonstrate a "W" in a different way?

    g. Allow students to brainstorm different ways to demonstrate other letters.

The word <u>together</u> is an important word to stress throughout this activity. Encourage students to generate one idea using a lot of letters and/or dots together, rather than multiple ideas for individual letters.

This is also a perfect opportunity to stress that no one should make fun of anyone else. Some of the world's greatest achievements have developed from the zaniest of ideas.

Occasionally act out an object for which a child has an idea. For example, if a child gives the idea of a butterfly made from a "B" and two black dots, tell all of the students to demonstrate how a butterfly may flit across the room. Tell them to show you the difference between a happy butterfly and a sad butterfly. Tell them to do this very slowly, and then do it quickly.

6. Once the book has been completed, ask the students to return to their desks or tables. As they return, encourage the singing of the "Alphabet Song."

7. At this point, recall some of the ideas presented during the reading of the story. Using an overhead projector, connect the cut-out letters and dots to demonstrate how they can form something new. Here are two sample ideas:

Alphabet

ABC
DEF
GHI

J K L
M N O
P Q R

S T U

V W

X Y Z

Divergent/Creative
Inventor Thinking
Small Group Lesson

Purpose

The purpose of this lesson is to apply **Inventor Thinking (divergent/creative think-ing),** which allows students to see extraordinary possibilities in ordinary, everyday items or situations. Remind students that:

❖ There are many correct responses/possibilities (**fluency**).

❖ Ideas may begin from a common "stem" but branch in different directions from there (**flexibility**).

❖ All ideas are welcomed, even those that seem silly at the time (**originality**).

❖ It is important to see things creatively which helps produce many possibilities in ordinary events, situations, and objects.

❖ It is encouraged to piggyback ideas on those from others (**elaboration**).

Materials

❖ One copy of the book <u>Ten Black Dots</u> by Donald Crews

❖ One copy of the book <u>Curious George's ABCs</u> by H.A. Rey

❖ Large white construction paper (one for each student)

❖ Glue stick (for teacher use)

❖ Permanent marker (for teacher use)

❖ Crayons

❖ *Alphabet* or die-cut letters (enough to provide each student with choices as needed)

❖ *Black Dots* or die-cut circles (enough for each student to use three or four in each creation)

❖ *Teacher Observation Checklist – Divergent/Creative Thinking*

Lesson Plan

1. Introduce the lesson by asking students to recall what an *inventor* is.

2. Next, hold up both books so students will recall the stories and examples presented during the previous two whole class lessons.

3. Tell the students that today they will brainstorm what can be made with a letter and number of dots of their choice.

4. Show students a sample that you have made (see sample below) using 2 As and 2 dots. Students must brainstorm a different idea than this one.

5. Allow students time to brainstorm individually.

6. Give each student the appropriate letter(s) and number of dot(s) needed for each idea. Stress that students MUST use at least one dot in each creation. It is important that the students connect the two stories together.

7. Once students have their letter(s) and dot(s) positioned on their papers, glue them down.

8. Students will connect the letter(s) and dot(s) together using crayons.

9. As they finish, have students explain their drawings. Ask if you may label the pictures, including "PETS – Divergent." Tell them that their parents will want to know that this project was completed for PETS. As noted below, this part of the activity is critical!

10. Record student ideas on the *Teacher Observation Checklist – Divergent/Creative Thinking.*

See samples of student work on the following page.

Please note the student work labeled as "steps." While most of the following samples are obvious, this student took an aerial view! The "N" was the first three steps and the two dots were stepping stones in the grass. At first glance, one may think that the student did not understand the assignment; therefore the explanation was critical.

Resources & Extensions*
Divergent/Creative Thinking

<u>Benny's Hat</u> by Linda Wagner Tyler & Dirk Walbrecker. (Atomium Books, 1991)

❖ Build divergent thinking skills by brainstorming more uses for Benny's hat.

<u>Challenging Projects for Creative Minds</u> by Phil and Dori Schlemmer. (Free Spirit Publishing, 1999)

❖ These activities encourage creating and inventing:
Animal Inventor
School Sign Company
American Heroes
Did You Know?

<u>Christina Katerina & the Box</u> by Patricia Lee Gauch. (Putnam & Grosset, 1998)

❖ Build divergent thinking skills by brainstorming more uses for cardboard boxes.

<u>Curious George's ABCs</u> by H.A. Rey. (Houghton Mifflin Company, 1998)

❖ Each letter in Curious George's version of the alphabet takes on a new persona through his creative drawings.

<u>The Discover! Series</u> by Greta & Ted Rasmussen. (Tin Man Press, 2001)

❖ These sets of cards offer young learners extraordinary experiences with everyday objects.

<u>If You Promise Not to Tell</u> by Joe Wayman. (Pieces of Learning, 1995)

❖ This collection of poems is an effective springboard for creative expression.

<u>In the Small, Small Pond</u> by Denise Fleming. (Henry Holt and Co., 1993)

- ❖ Life in a small pond is explored through a delightful dance of descriptive vocabulary.

<u>Meggie Moon</u> by Elizabeth Baguley. (Scholastic, Inc., 2005)

- ❖ What can be done with a yard full of trash? Two boys discover its potential when Meggie Moon comes to visit.

<u>Not A Box</u> by Antoinette Portis. (HarperCollins, 2006)

- ❖ A rabbit cleverly shares his visions of what a simple cardboard box could be to him.

<u>One Mitten </u>by Kristine O'Connell. (Clarion Books, 2005)

- ❖ Find out all the things you can do with one mitten or two in this clever book.

<u>Primarily Thinking</u> by Judy Leimbach. (Prufrock Press, 2005)

- ❖ The open-ended brainstorming activities encourage creative thinking.

<u>That's My Dog</u> by Rick Walton. (Putnam, 2001)

- ❖ Experience sentence expansion at its most creative -- beginning with "A big red dog" and adding a word at a time to achieve: "He's my big, red, happy, muddy, smart, bouncy, slobbery, sneaky, stinky dog!"

<u>The Secret </u>by Lindsay George Barrett. (Greenwillow, 2005)

- ❖ The forest animals have a secret they whisper to one another. Expressive, creative synonyms are used for "talking."

<u>The Sound of Day, The Sound of Night</u> by Mary O'Neill. (Farrar, 2003)

- ❖ What are day sounds? What are night sounds? Brainstorm other possibilities.

<u>Surprise in the Middle</u> by Greta & Ted Rasmussen. (Tin Man Press, 2001)

  ❖ Convergent, divergent, and visual directions are used as clues in these activities in order to create a drawing. They encourage active listening and attention to details.

<u>Ten Black Dots</u> by Donald Crews. (Harper Trophy, 1995)

  ❖ What can be made from different numbers of dots?

<u>Things that are most in the world</u> by Judi Barrett. (Aladdin Paperbacks, 2001)

  ❖ What is the wiggliest thing in the world? A snake ice-skating! What's the silliest … the quietest … the prickliest???

<u>Three Pebbles and a Song</u> by Eileen Spinelli. (Dial, 2003)

  ❖ A small mouse sets out to gather things for winter but the things he brings home seem useless … or are they?

<u>What's What: A Guessing Game</u> by Mary Serfozo. (Trade Paperbacks, 2000)

  ❖ Use divergent thinking to brainstorm things with certain attributes, like soft and hard, as this poem unfolds.

***Note:** Too quickly, too often, really great books go unexpectedly out of print. Should you choose a resource that has suffered this sad fate, be sure to check out the second-hand booksellers at Amazon.com as many such titles may still be available through them.

Questions That Encourage
Divergent/Creative Thinking

Following are two generic sets of questions designed to reinforce the divergent/creative thinking skills identified with each question. Use them with any extension resources. The questions are presented in three formats:

- In a list with specific thinking skills and some suggested applications filled in;

- On strips to copy and cut apart for flexibility of use – in random order or in a planned sequence; and

- On Q'ubes™ -- question cubes that students can toss and roll for a more active, kinesthetic involvement in the questioning process.

There are two tiers of questions. The first Tier of questions includes those that are simpler and less open-ended than the questions in Tier 2 in order to allow you to differentiate for different readiness levels in your students.

Encourage your students to pose their own questions for others in the class to answer. According to Socrates and John Dewey, a lot more thinking goes into such "active" questioning than into answering questions.

The Questions
Tier 1

What might happen if …?
- Flexibility of thought: re-organization
- What might happen if *[change any factor in the story – characters, setting, plot]*?

If you were __________ in the story, what would you do differently?
- Flexibility of thought: involvement
- If you were *[any character]* in the story, what would you do differently?

How would <u>you</u> end this story differently?
- Flexibility of thought: re-organization
- Originality

How does __________ feel about what's happening in the story?
- Flexibility of thought: involvement, viewpoint
- Imagine being *[any character in the story]*: How does *[that character]* feel about what's happening in the story?

In how many different ways could you describe __________?
- Fluency of thought
- Elaboration
- In how many different ways could you describe *[a character in the story]*?
- In how many different ways could you describe *[a place in the story]*?
- In how many different ways could you describe *[an object in the story]*?

What else could __________ have done?
- Flexibility of thought: re-organization
- What else could *[any character in the story]* have done?

The Questions
Tier 2

How many different ways could you end this story?
- Fluency of thought
- Flexibility of thought: re-organization

If you were ______________, how would you tell this story?
- Flexibility of thought: involvement, viewpoint
- If you were *[any character who has not been the main voice of the story]*, how would you tell this story?

How would this story be different if it took place in ___________?
- Flexibility of thought: re-organization
- How would this story be different if it took place in *[your neighborhood]*?
- How would this story be different if it took place in *[name another country]*?
- How would this story be different if it took place *[in a forest/at the beach/on a mountain top/etc.]*?

How would this story be different if it happened in the past/future?
- Flexibility of thought: re-organization

How many other things could __________ have done?
- Fluency of thought
- Flexibility of thought: re-organization
- How many other things could *[a character in the story]* have done?

If you could talk to ______________, what would you say?
- Flexibility of thought: conscious self-deception/creative pretence
- If you could talk to *[any character in the story]*, what would you say?

What might happen if ... ?

If you were _________ in the story, what would you do differently?

How would you end this story differently?

How does _______ feel about what's happening in the story?

In how many different ways could you describe _______?

What else could _______ have done?

How many different ways could you end this story?

If you were __________, how would you tell this story?

How would this story be different if it took place in __________ ?

How would this story be different if it happened in the past/future?

How many other things could __________ have done?

If you could talk to __________, what would you say?

A PETS™ Q'UBE
Divergent/Creative Thinking

Tier 1

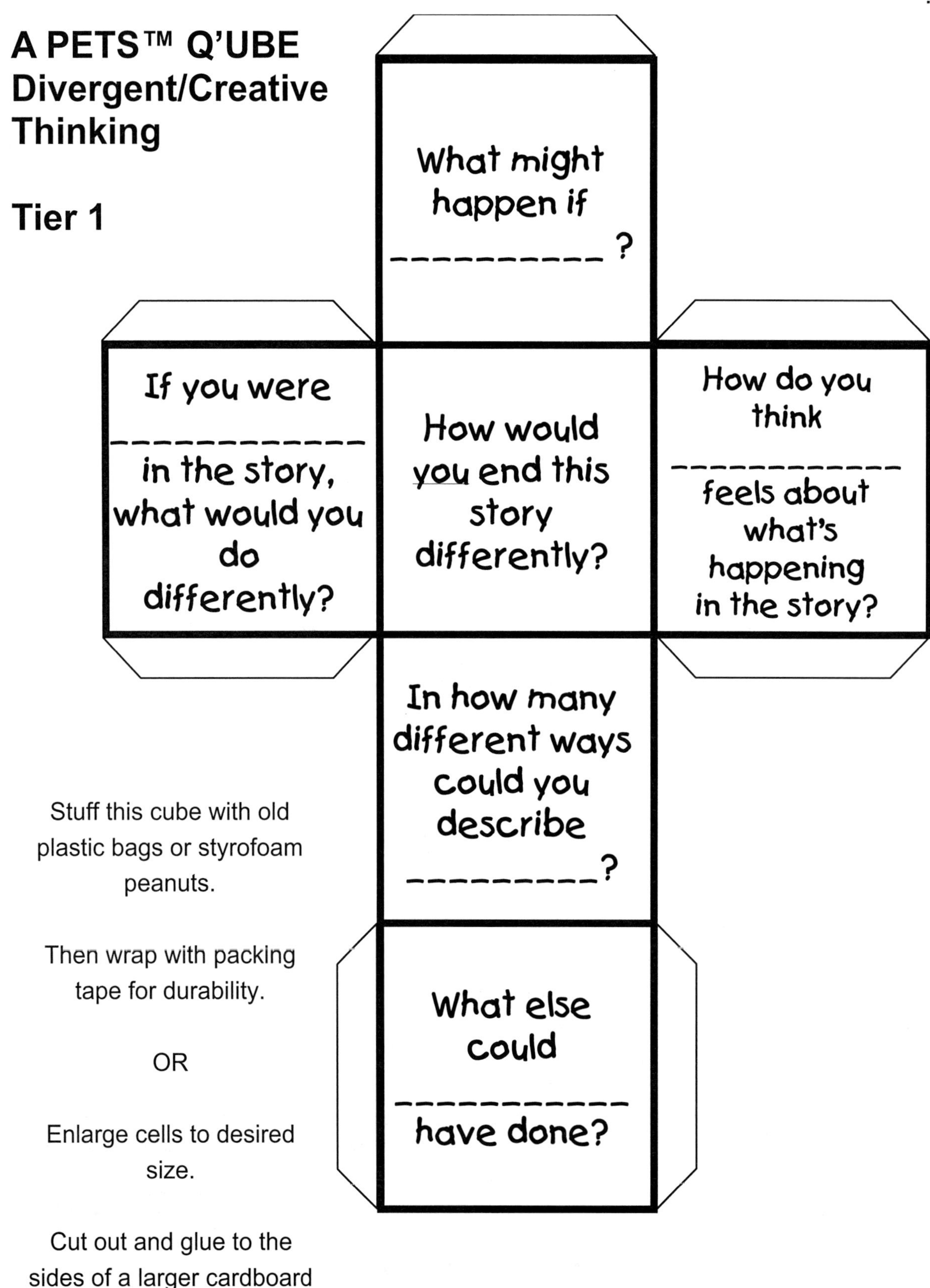

Stuff this cube with old plastic bags or styrofoam peanuts.

Then wrap with packing tape for durability.

OR

Enlarge cells to desired size.

Cut out and glue to the sides of a larger cardboard box.

A PETS™ Q'UBE
Divergent/Creative Thinking

Tier 2

How many different ways could you end this story?

How would you tell this story from the point of view of ___________ ?

How would this story be different if it took place in ___________ ?

How would this story be different if it happened in the past/ future?

How many other things could ________ have done?

If you could talk to ___________, what would you say?

Stuff this cube with old plastic bags or styrofoam peanuts.

Then wrap with packing tape for durability.

OR

Enlarge cells to desired size.

Cut out and glue to the sides of a larger cardboard box.

Notes

Convergent/Analytical Thinking

During each lesson, the teacher and observer are looking for students who demonstrate logical deductive reasoning by identifying and using clues to determine the correct solution to a problem. They tend to see the interrelationships between clues and defer judgment until all clues have been collected. Many times they will display outside knowledge about a topic that will help them discover the solution. The ability to see intuitively the correct answer is another characteristic of students who excel at convergent/analytical thinking. Students who display much enthusiasm during the activity should be observed carefully as well.

Diagnostic Notes

An observation checklist is provided. Use the same checklist for both whole class and small group lessons. This way all of the data is together on one sheet. The following is a short summary of what to look for in student behaviors:

USES CLUES EFFECTIVELY – Look for students who are able to quickly understand and use clues to determine the answer. Note students who are the first to figure out a correct answer. Look for students who see how to build one clue's information on a previous clue to deduce the answer.

RECOGNIZES ATTRIBUTES – Look for students who are aware of details. They see similarities and differences that may be used as clues. Note students who categorize or sort in unusual or different ways. These students come up with ideas that few other students think of.

DRAWS RELATIONSHIPS – Look for students who exhibit knowledge from outside the classroom and use it as an additional clue in solving the story. Note students who see the relationship between convergent thinking and other classroom activities.

RECOGNIZES FLAWED REASONING – Look for students who are able to recognize when a certain sorting system or application of clues will not work.

DEMONSTRATES PERSEVERANCE – Look for students who are willing to wait until they have figured out the correct answer. These students avoid guessing until they determine the correct answer. These are also the students who work to figure out the solution regardless of how long it takes.

INTUITIVELY SEES ANSWER – Some students who are excellent convergent thinkers are unable to verbalize how they figured out the answer. Note students when this occurs.

Kindergarten PETS -- Teacher Observation Checklist
CONVERGENT/ANALYTICAL THINKING

Teacher: School Year:

Student Names	Uses Clues Effectively	Recognizes Attributes	Draws Relationships	Recognizes Flawed Reasoning	Demonstrates Perseverance	Intuitively Sees Answers	Teacher Observations	TOTALS

Convergent/Analytical
Detective Thinking
Whole Class
Lesson 1

Purpose

The purpose of this lesson is to introduce the concepts of **Detective Thinking (convergent/analytical deduction)** that puts clues together in order to <u>deduce</u> the one correct answer to the problem. Students will listen for clues in a story in order to determine that correct answer. Convergent/analytical thinking focuses on the following concepts:

- ❖ There is one and only one right answer to these problems.

- ❖ Students may need to put together many pieces of information in order to find the one right answer.

- ❖ Attributes are important clues.

- ❖ Students may feel like saying *"I have it!"* when they find the answer.

- ❖ Students may not see the answer right away and need to reflect on some of the clues.

- ❖ Patience is important in not jumping to conclusions and in reflecting on clues.

Materials

- ❖ One copy of the book <u>How Will We Get to the Beach?</u> by Brigitte Luciani and Eve Tharlet (classroom-sized books are best, if available)

- ❖ An overhead projector or chalkboard

- ❖ An overhead transparency of *What Does Not Fit In?* Cut the transparency into four strips that separate the four groups of items.

- ❖ *Teacher Observation Checklist – Convergent/Analytical Thinking*

Lesson Plan

1. Introduce the lesson by asking how many students are good detectives. Explain that everyone can look and listen for clues in order to solve a mystery or problem.

2. It is important that Kindergarteners continue to change venues, so at this point ask them to move to a reading area in which to share the story. This way all students can also see the pictures clearly.

3. During the activity below, the classroom teacher will gather data on the *Teacher Observation Checklist – Convergent/Analytical Thinking* provided with each student's name on it.

4. Begin to read the story pausing at each page for responses. When a student gives a response, have each explain what the clue was that prompted that idea. Have students explain other items that may be reasonable responses (deductive reasoning).

This is also a perfect opportunity to remind students that as we learned in the last thinking strategy, <u>no</u> one's ideas are silly or should be laughed at. Putting clues together correctly can sometimes be tricky.

5. Once the book has been completed, ask the students to return to their desks or tables. At this point, put the *What Does Not Fit In?* groups of pictures on the overhead projector. Ask students to determine which item does not fit in with the rest of the group. Have them explain what clue or clues indicate this. For example:

Group 1:   blanket   picnic basket   ants   snow boots

(ANSWER: "Snow boots" do not fit because all others are things from a picnic.)

Group 2:   grass   trees   cardinal   frog

(ANSWER: "Cardinal" does not fit because all others are green things.)

Group 3:   dog   car   cat   can

(ANSWER: "Dog" does not fit because all others are words starting with "C.")

Group 4:   dog   cat   car   apple

(ANSWER: "Apple" does not fit because all others are three-letter words.)

What Does Not Fit In?

Convergent/Analytical
Detective Thinking
Whole Class
Lesson 2

Purpose

The purpose of this lesson is to reinforce **Detective Thinking (convergent/analytical deduction)** that puts clues together in order to <u>deduce</u> the one correct answer to the problem. Students will listen for clues in a story in order to determine that correct answer. Convergent/analytical thinking focuses on the following concepts:

- ❖ There is one and only one right answer to these problems.

- ❖ Students may need to put together many pieces of information in order to find the one right answer.

- ❖ Attributes are important clues.

- ❖ Students may feel like saying *"I have it!"* when they find the answer.

- ❖ Students may not see the answer right away and need to reflect on some of the clues.

- ❖ Patience is important in not jumping to conclusions and in reflecting on clues.

Materials

- ❖ One copy of the book <u>Brown Bear, Brown Bear, What Do You See?</u> by Bill Martin, Jr. (classroom-sized books are best, if available)

- ❖ An overhead projector or chalkboard

- ❖ *Observation Checklist – Convergent/Analytical Thinking*

Lesson Plan

1. Introduce the lesson by asking how many students have ever found something in the dark that made them frightened until they used their detective thinking to determine what the object truly was.

2. Tell the students that they will now be hearing a story in which they will be determining creatures based only on color clues.

3. It is important that Kindergarteners continue to change venues, so at this point ask them to move to a reading area in which to share the story. This way all students can also see the pictures clearly.

4. During the activity below, the classroom teacher will gather data on the *Teacher Observation Checklist – Convergent/Analytical Thinking* provided with each student's name on it.

5. Begin to read <u>Brown Bear, Brown Bear, What Do You See?</u> by Bill Martin, Jr. <u>However</u>, substitute a mystery statement to be solved while not revealing ANY of the right-hand side pages. Read in a singsong fashion allowing students to join in when they feel comfortable doing so. For example:

Read:	*"Brown Bear, Brown Bear, What do you see?*
But <u>instead of</u> reading:	"I see a red bird looking at me."
Say:	*"I see <u>something red flying</u> at me."*
Pause for responses.	

Read:	*"Red Bird, Red Bird, What do you see?"*
But <u>instead of</u> reading:	"I see a yellow duck looking at me."
Say:	*"I see <u>something yellow walking</u> toward me."*
Pause for responses.	

Continue in this fashion, reading only the initial question for each animal, adding a color clue statement, and then pausing for student responses. Following are possible color and behavior clues for the other animals in the book:

Blue horse Pause for responses.	*"I see <u>something blue galloping</u> toward me."*
Green frog Pause for responses.	*"I see <u>something green</u> looking at me."*
Purple cat Pause for responses.	*"I see <u>something purple purring</u> at me."*

| White dog | *"I see <u>something white</u> looking at me."* |
| Pause for responses. | |

| Black sheep | *"I see <u>something black</u> following me."* |
| Pause for responses. | |

| Goldfish | *"I see <u>something gold</u> staring at me."* |
| Pause for responses. | |

| Teacher | *"I see <u>someONE</u> smiling at me."* |
| Pause for responses. | |

| Read: | *"Teacher, Teacher, What do you see?* (addressing the classroom teacher) |
| The teacher responds: | *"I see children looking at me!"* |

| Read: | *"Children, Children, What do you see?"* |

Open to the last two pages of the book, point to each, and allow children to recite each animal back before finishing with:

"And a teacher looking at us. That's what WE see!"

Students use the color clues to determine what each creature sees. When the color does not match the creature, students must use other types of clues to determine the creature. Be sure NOT to show the page of the creature until all students have shared their conclusions. Also allow students to correct flawed ideas without diminishing another student's idea.

This is also a perfect opportunity to remind students that, as we learned while doing Inventor Thinking, <u>no</u> one's ideas are silly or should be laughed at. Putting clues together correctly can sometimes be tricky.

6. Between questions, encourage divergent brainstorming and creative movement by asking students to role play the animal under consideration. For example:

| Ask: | *"Can you show us what a green frog looks like?* |
| Then: | *"What about a blue frog?" "Where might you find a blue frog?"* |

| Ask: | *"Can you show us what a black sheep looks like? How about a white sheep?"* |
| Then: | *"What's the difference?"* |

7. Once the book has been completed, ask the students to return to their desks or tables. At this point, recall some of the conclusions generated during the story, particularly any unusual responses. Then discuss how some creatures may have more than one color, demonstrating different ways of applying the clues. Record these ideas on the overhead projector or chalkboard.

8. Bring closure to the lesson by role-playing some of the creatures from the story. For example, say to students:

   ❖ *"Show me your best white wolf impression."*
   ❖ *"Show me your best gray wolf impression."*
   ❖ Discuss similarities and differences between the impressions.
   ❖ Ask them, *"What clues besides color can help you identify each animal?"*

Convergent/Analytical
Detective Thinking
Small Group Lesson

Purpose

The purpose of this lesson is to apply **Detective Thinking (convergent/analytical deduction)** by putting clues together to <u>deduce</u> the one correct answer to the problem. Students will also classify and organize information collected. Remind students that:

❖ There is one and only one right answer to these problems.

❖ They may need to put together many pieces of information in order to find the one right answer.

❖ Attributes are important clues.

❖ They may feel like saying *"I have it!"* when they find the answer.

❖ They may not see the answer right away and need to reflect on some of the clues.

❖ Patience is important in not jumping to conclusions and in reflecting on clues.

Materials

❖ One set of *Mystery Animal Cards* (black & white) for EACH student PLUS an additional set for the teacher (lamination recommended for use year after year)

❖ One set of *Mystery Person Cards* (color) for EACH student PLUS an additional set for the teacher (lamination recommended for use year after year)

<u>**Coloring Key:**</u>

Schoolgirl must have **brown hair.**
All others must have **blonde hair.**
Cowgirl must be wearing things that are **green.**
Judge must have **no green** on.

❖ *Teacher Observation Checklist – Convergent/Analytical Thinking*

Lesson Plan

1. Begin with the Mystery Animals Cards, which happen to be the characters from the PETS™ 123 program. You do not need to point this out. Go over each card so that you are sure that each child has all six correct cards AND so that you are sure that each child knows what animals are being portrayed on each card.

2. Tell the students that they will hold all six cards in their hands so no one else can see their cards. It is not necessary that they fan them like a normal hand of cards. They may simply hold them as a single stack.

3. As you give clues, tell the students to select the card or cards that do not fit that clue and put them in a discard pile in front of them FACE DOWN.

4. Begin by reading the first clue. Give students plenty of time to reason through each card to determine if it stays or is discarded. The first clue may be guided. For example, say, *"I have fur."* Then point out that any animal that does NOT have fur should be discarded.

6. Continue reading the clues until all have been read:

> ❖ I have fur.
> ❖ I *don't* hop.
> ❖ I *don't* eat nuts.

ANSWER: Dog (Dudley the Detective)

7. Once all clues have been read, students should have only one card left, and it should be the Mystery Animal. If some students still have more than one card, read the clues again to eliminate more cards. Suggest to any students who think they already have the answer that they listen to the clues again to double-check their work.

7. If any students still have more than one card at this point, be patient. Ask them if they need to hear the clues again. Remember, this may be a student who is deferring judgment by reviewing all the clues mentally.

8. Students will reveal their remaining cards all at the same time once each student has one and only one card left. This will reduce the chance of copying.

9. Record student responses on the *Teacher Observation Checklist – Convergent/Analytical Thinking.*

10. Repeat the process using the Mystery Person Card Set. This set adds the attribute of color.

> ❖ I have blonde hair.
> ❖ I *don't* like hot places.
> ❖ I am *not* wearing any jewelry.
> ❖ I am *not* wearing green.

ANSWER: Judge

11. Record student responses on the *Teacher Observation Checklist – Convergent/Analytical Thinking.*

12. Time will determine how many rounds are played with each deck. A blank clue is included so that students can devise their own clues.

ANSWER KEY:

Mystery Animal #1 – Dog (Dudley the Detective)

Mystery Animal #2 – Kangaroo (Sybil the Scientist)

Mystery Animal #3 – Owl (Jordan the Judge)

Mystery Person #1 – Judge

Mystery Person #2 – Indian

Mystery Person #3 – Judge

Mystery Animal Card Set
(May remain black & white images)

Mystery Person Card Set

(Must be colored according to Key)

Clue Cards

MYSTERY ANIMAL #1
- ❖ I have fur.
- ❖ I *don't* hop.
- ❖ I *don't* eat nuts.

MYSTERY PERSON #1
- ❖ I have blond hair.
- ❖ I *don't* like hot places.
- ❖ I am *not* wearing any jewelry.
- ❖ I am *not* wearing green.

MYSTERY ANIMAL #2
- ❖ I hop.
- ❖ I DON'T walk on four legs.
- ❖ I like science.

MYSTERY PERSON #2
- ❖ I have something on my head.
- ❖ I am NOT wearing a belt.
- ❖ I am NOT wearing a number.

MYSTERY ANIMAL #3
- ❖ I DON'T have fur.
- ❖ I am wise.
- ❖ I can fly.

MYSTERY PERSON #3
- ❖ I have short hair.
- ❖ I am NOT wearing anything on my head.
- ❖ I am NOT wearing glasses.
- ❖ I am wearing long pants.

MYSTERY ANIMAL
1. _______________
2. _______________
3. _______________
4. _______________

MYSTERY PERSON
1. _______________
2. _______________
3. _______________
4. _______________

Resources & Extensions*
Convergent/Analytical Thinking

<u>Analogies for Beginners</u> by Dianne Draze. (Prufrock Press, 1989)

> ❖ These analogies require students to analyze the elements of each puzzle, define relationships, and apply those relationships. Flexible and critical thinking are involved when completing the verbal activities in this book.

<u>Are You There, Bear?</u> by Ron Maris. (Puffin Picture Book, 1986)

> ❖ In a darkened bedroom, several toys search for a hidden bear.

<u>Attribute Logic Block Activities</u> by Don Balka. (Ideal School Supply Co., 1985)

> ❖ These puzzles use Venn diagrams and attribute blocks to reinforce convergent thinking strategies.

<u>Brown Bear, Brown Bear, What Do You See?</u> by Bill Martin, Jr. (Henry Holt & Co., 1996)

> ❖ So many things are looking at Brown Bear – can you guess what they are from the color clues?

<u>Disney's Mickey & Friends Activity Workbook</u> by Disney Enterprises, Inc. (Modern Publishing, 1998)

> ❖ Activity pages in this book combine convergent and visual thinking by presenting outlines as clues in order to determine missing objects.

<u>First Time Analogies</u> by Dianne Draze. (Prufrock Press, 2005)

> ❖ These analogy activities are divided into four sections, each one presenting analogies with different formats and degrees of difficulty.

<u>Guess Where I Live</u> by Anni Axworthy. (Walker Books, 1999)

❖ In this peep-hole book, students find clues to determine where different kinds of animals live.

<u>How Will We Get to the Beach?</u> by Brigitte Luciani and Eve Tharlet. (North-South Books, 2003)

❖ What clues can be found that help determine how this family gets to the beach.

<u>In the Garden: Who's Been Here?</u> by Lindsay Barrett George (Greenwillow, 2006)
<u>In the Woods: Who's Been Here?</u> by Lindsay Barrett George (Greenwillow, 1995)

❖ Who are the animal interlopers in the garden and the woods? What clues have they left behind that give them away?

<u>It Wasn't Me!</u> by Udo Weigelt. (North-South Books, 2001)

❖ When Ferret's raspberries are missing, his friends try to find out who did it!

<u>Mystery Mansion</u>, by Michael Garland. (Dutton Children's Books, 2001)

❖ As Tommy follows his aunt's clues to a mysterious surprise, he's surrounded by animals and letters – can you find them all?

<u>Polar Bear, Polar Bear, What Do You Hear?</u> by Bill Martin, Jr. (Henry Holt and Co., 1991)

❖ Each animal hears the next animal – can students connect animal sounds to the correct animal?

<u>Primarily Thinking</u> by Judy Leimbach. (Prufrock Press, 2005)

❖ The classification activities encourage students to determine the common qualities or properties of several items.
❖ Cause & effect activities present relationships in which one incident causes something else to happen.

<u>Surprise in the Middle</u> by Greta and Ted Rasmussen. (Tin Man Press, 2001)

> ❖ These activities combine convergent, divergent, and visual directions used as clues in order to create drawings. They encourage active listening and attention to details.

<u>Who Stole the Gold?</u> by Udo Weigelt & J. Gukova. (North-South Books, 2000)

> ❖ A mystery has to be solved when Hamster's gold is missing and all the forest suspects claim to be innocent.

***Note:** Too quickly, too often, really great books go unexpectedly out of print. Should you choose a resource that has suffered this sad fate, be sure to check out the second-hand booksellers at Amazon.com as many such titles may still be available through them.

Questions That Encourage Convergent/Analytical Thinking

Following are two generic sets of questions designed to reinforce the convergent/ analytical thinking skills identified with each question. Use them with any extension resources. The questions are presented in three formats:

- In a list with specific thinking skills and some suggested applications filled in;

- On strips to copy and cut apart for flexibility of use – in random order or in a planned sequence; and

- On Q'ubes™ -- question cubes that students can toss and roll for a more active, kinesthetic involvement in the questioning process.

There are two tiers of questions. The first Tier of questions includes those that are simpler and less open-ended than the questions in Tier 2 in order to allow you to differentiate for different readiness levels in your students.

Encourage your students to pose their own questions for others in the class to answer. According to Socrates and John Dewey, a lot more thinking goes into such "active" questioning than into answering questions.

The Questions
Tier 1

What caused __________ to happen?
- Cause and effect
- What caused *[an event in the story]* to happen?

How are _________ and _________ alike?
- Compare
- Patterns and relationships
- Attributes: examining parts of the whole
- How are *[a character from the story]* and *[another character from this story or another story read in class]* alike?
- How are *[a place in the story]* and *[a place in another story or in the real world like your neighborhood]* alike?

How are _________ and _________ different?
- Contrast
- Attributes: examining parts of the whole
- How are *[a character from the story]* and *[another character from this story or another story read in class]* different?
- How are *[a place in the story]* and *[a place in another story or in the real world like your neighborhood]* different?

What is something you do or feel that is like _________?
- Compare
- Pattern and relationships
- What is something you do or feel that is like *[a character in the story]*?

What clues helped you solve the problem (or mystery) in the story?
- Identifying pertinent information
- Deductive reasoning

What kinds of __________ did you find in this story?
- Classification
- What kinds of *[animals]* did you find in this story?
- What kinds of *[plants]* did you find in this story?
- What kinds of *[community workers]* did you find in this story?

The Questions
Tier 2

Think of something that happened in the story. What caused it?
- Cause and effect

In how many ways are _______________ and _____________ alike and/or different?
- Compare and contrast
- Fluency of thought (divergent thinking)
- In how many ways are *[a character in the story]* and *[another character in this story or another story read in class]* alike and/or different?

In how many ways are <u>you</u> and ____________ alike and/or different?
- Compare and contrast
- Fluency of thought (divergent thinking)
- In how many ways are <u>you</u> and *[a character in this story]* alike and/or different?

What parts of the story may not be "real?" What parts are real? How do you know?
- Examining parts of the whole
- Fact versus fiction

What is the message in this story? What other stories have a similar message?
- Identifying pertinent information
- Drawing inferences
- Inductive reasoning

What do you think would happen next in the story if it continued?
- Prediction

What caused __________ to happen?

How are _____ and _____ alike?

How are _____ and _____ different?

What is something you do or feel that is like __________ ?

What clues helped you solve the problem (or mystery) in the story?

What kinds of _______ did you find in this story?

Think of something that happened in the story. What caused it?
In how many ways are _____ and _____ alike and/or different?
In how many ways are <u>you</u> and _____ alike and/or different?
What parts of the story may not be "real?" What parts are real? How do you know?
What is the message in this story? What other stories have a similar message?
What do you think would happen next in the story if it continued?

A PETS™ Q'UBE
Convergent/ Analytical Thinking

Tier 1

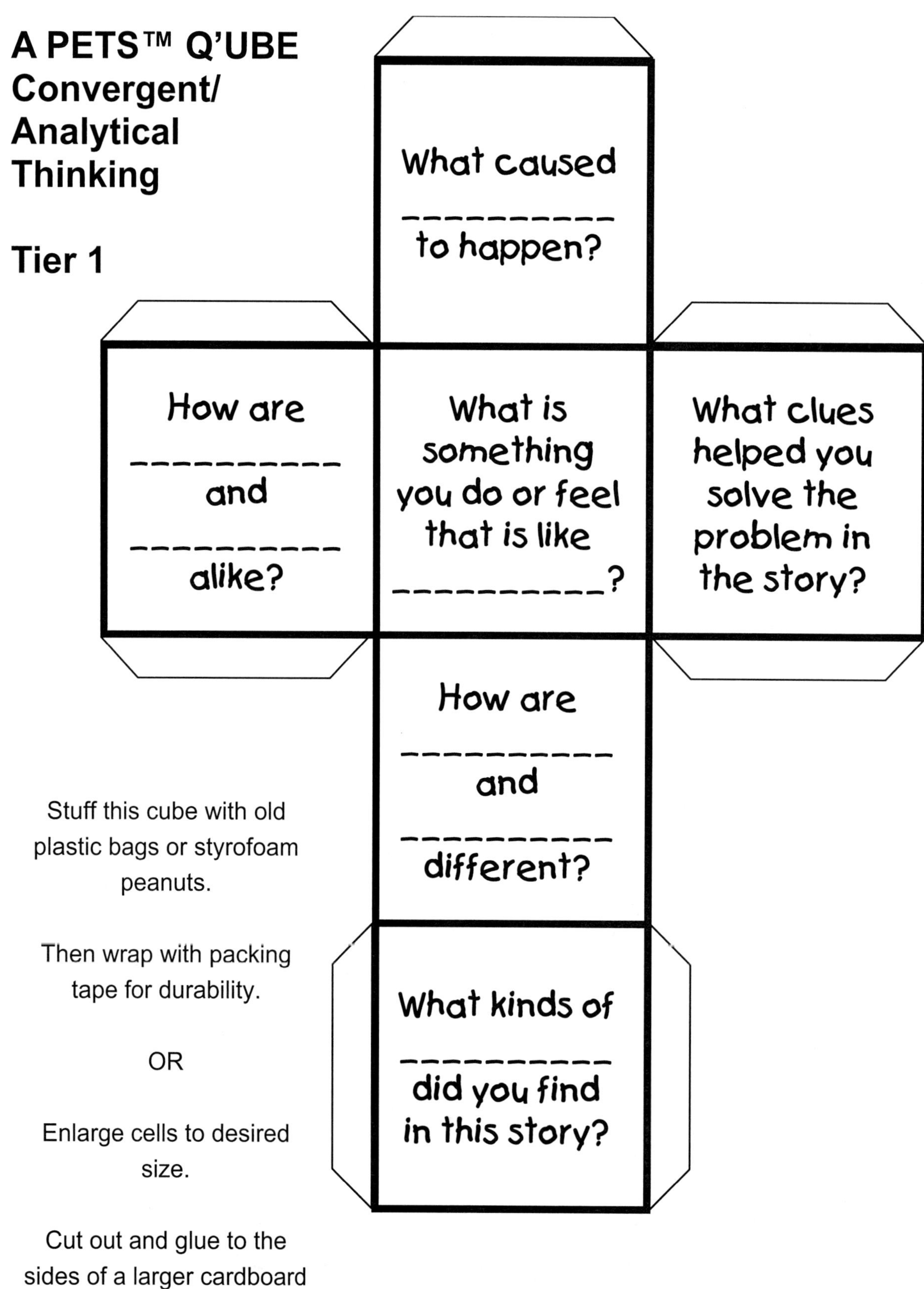

Stuff this cube with old plastic bags or styrofoam peanuts.

Then wrap with packing tape for durability.

OR

Enlarge cells to desired size.

Cut out and glue to the sides of a larger cardboard box.

A PETS™ Q'UBE
Convergent/
Analytical
Thinking

Tier 2

Think of something that happened in the story. What caused it?

In how many ways are you and ___________ alike and/or different?

In how many ways are _______ and _________ alike and/or different?

What parts of the story may not be "real"? What parts are real? How do you know?

What is the message in the story? What other stories have a similar message?

What do you think would happen next in the story if it continued?

Stuff this cube with old plastic bags or styrofoam peanuts.

Then wrap with packing tape for durability.

OR

Enlarge cells to desired size.

Cut out and glue to the sides of a larger cardboard box.

<u>Notes</u>

Visual/Spatial Thinking

During the whole class lesson, the teacher and observer are looking for students who are able to manipulate shapes mentally in order to achieve a solution. These students have good memories for visual details. They often enjoy activities involving hands-on building of three-dimensional objects. Since these students may not be as verbal as their classmates, they may not have as much opportunity to demonstrate their talents during traditional classroom activities. They often respond best to visual images such as graphic organizers and instructional computer programs. Students who display much enthusiasm during the activity should be observed carefully as well as those who elaborate on their own ideas or on the ideas of others.

Diagnostic Notes

An observation checklist is provided. Use the same checklist for both whole class and small group lessons so that all of the data is together on one sheet. The following is a short summary of what to look for in student behaviors:

GRASPS CONCEPTS QUICKLY – Look for students who quickly see the perceptions presented. If they need to be shown a "trick," such as turning a pattern block, note those students who remember that "trick" and will try it in other situations.

SEES INTERRELATIONSHIP OF CLUES – Look for students who will use all available clues or ideas to try to figure out the pattern.

MANIPULATES SHAPES MENTALLY – Sometimes the teacher will be able to observe the students as they turn their heads or hands, trying to visualize or manipulate an object or thought.

DEFERS JUDGEMENT – These students will wait to answer rather than jump to a wrong conclusion.

DEMONSTRATES PERSEVERANCE – Look for students who are willing to wait until they have figured out the correct answer. These students avoid guessing until they determine the correct answer. These are also the students who work to figure out the solution regardless of how long it takes.

INTUITIVELY SEES ANSWER – Look for students who seem to understand intuitively the visual perceptions presented. They may have the correct answer without knowing how they got that answer.

Kindergarten PETS -- Teacher Observation Checklist
VISUAL/SPATIAL THINKING

Teacher:

School Year:

Student Names	Grasps Concepts Quickly	Manipulates Shapes Mentally	Sees Interrelationship of Clues	Defers Judgment	Demonstrates Perseverance	Intuitively Sees Answers	Teacher Observations	TOTALS

Visual/Spatial
Magician Thinking
Whole Class
Lesson 1

Purpose

The purpose of this lesson is to introduce students to **Magician Thinking (visual/ spatial perception)**. These activities, like a magician, will attempt to "fool our brains" through what our eyes perceive. Combining previously learned thinking skills in analyzing spatial relationships and reconstructing the parts into new wholes, visual/spatial thinking focuses on the following concepts:

- ❖ Thinking skills do not occur in isolation; spatial perception activities use both convergent and divergent thinking strategies.

- ❖ Shapes can be manipulated mentally without concrete devices.

- ❖ Visual patterns are predictable.

- ❖ The eyes and the brain must work together to "think" about given information.

- ❖ Tolerance for ambiguity and perseverance are essential components for flexible, high-level visual thinking.

Materials

- ❖ One copy of the book <u>Seven Blind Mice</u> by Ed Young (classroom-sized books are best)

- ❖ An overhead projector or chalkboard

- ❖ *Teacher Observation Checklist – Visual/Spatial Thinking*

Lesson Plan

1. Introduce the lesson by asking students if they have ever thought about what it would be like to be blind. Allow time for discussion, and then tell the students that they will get a chance to feel what it would be like as you read the story today. Talk briefly about what "visual" means and how people can "visualize" without actually seeing:

   > Visual – Something that can be seen using your eyes.
   > Visualize – To form a mental picture of something in your mind.

2. Tell the students that they will be hearing a story that is about seven blind mice. Tell them that as you read the story you will give them a chance to guess each item being described by the blind mice BEFORE seeing the pictures.

3. It is important that Kindergarteners continue to change venues, so ask them to move to a reading area in which to share the story. This way all students can also see the pictures clearly.

4. During the activity below, the classroom teacher will gather data on the *Teacher Observation Checklist – Visual/Spatial Thinking* provided with each student's name on it.

5. Begin to read <u>Seven Blind Mice</u> by Ed Young. Once you read each page, ask students if they can tell what the object may be based only on its description.

This is also a perfect opportunity to remind students that as previously learned, no one's ideas are silly nor should they be laughed at.

6. Once the book has been completed, ask the students to return to their desks or tables. At this point, review some of the ideas presented during the reading of the story, and have a small discussion of how certain objects may appear differently if you were blind. You can record these ideas on the overhead projector or chalkboard. You can use small words or pictures to show ideas.

   © Pieces of Learning

Visual/Spatial
Magician Thinking
Whole Class
Lesson 2

Purpose

The purpose of this lesson is to reinforce **Magician Thinking (visual/spatial perception)**. These activities, like a magician, will attempt to "fool our brains" through what our eyes perceive. Combining previously learned thinking skills in analyzing spatial relationships and reconstructing the parts into new wholes, visual/spatial thinking focuses on the following concepts:

- ❖ Thinking skills do not occur in isolation; spatial perception activities use both convergent and divergent thinking strategies.

- ❖ Shapes can be manipulated mentally without concrete devices.

- ❖ Visual patterns are predictable.

- ❖ The eyes and the brain must work together to "think" about given information.

- ❖ Tolerance for ambiguity and perseverance are essential components for flexible, high-level visual thinking.

Materials

- ❖ One copy of the book <u>When a Line Bends … A Shape Begins</u> by Rhonda Gowler Greene (classroom-sized books are best)

- ❖ An overhead projector or chalkboard

- ❖ An overhead transparency of *Shaping Up.* Cut out the different shapes to manipulate individually on the overhead projector.

- ❖ *Teacher Observation Checklist – Visual/Spatial Thinking*

Lesson Plan

1. Introduce the lesson by reviewing "visualization." Explain how people can manipulate shapes in their minds through visualization. Tell the students that they will get a chance to manipulate shapes in their minds as you read the story today.

2. It is important that Kindergarteners continue to change venues, so at this point ask them to move to a reading area in which to share the story. This way all students can clearly see the pictures as well.

3. During the activity below, the classroom teacher will gather data on the *Teacher Observation Checklist – Visual/Spatial Thinking* provided with each student's name on it.

4. Begin to read <u>When a Line Bends, a Shape Begins</u> by Rhonda Growler. Once you read each page, ask students to think of other objects that are made using that shape.

This is also a perfect opportunity to remind students that as we learned in past thinking strategies, <u>no</u> one's ideas are silly or should be laughed at.

5. Once the book has been completed, ask the students to return to their desks or tables. At this point, place a *Shaping Up!* shape on the overhead projector (or draw one on the chalkboard) for students to manipulate mentally in order to form something new. *You may wish to keep a copy of these for recall during small group sessions.* Here are a few examples you may start with:

Combine: ○ with ♔ to get (king)

○ with ☼ to get (sun)

○ with ▲▲ to get (cat)

○ with ∘ ∘ to get (bear or mouse)

Shaping Up!

Visual/Spatial
Magician Thinking
Small Group Lesson

Purpose

The purpose of this lesson is to apply **Magician Thinking (visual/spatial perception)**. These activities will attempt to "fool our brains" through what our eyes perceive and will combine analyzing spatial relationships with reconstructing the parts into new wholes. Remind students that:

❖ Thinking skills do not occur in isolation -- spatial perception activities use both convergent and divergent thinking strategies.

❖ Shapes can be manipulated mentally without concrete devices.

❖ Visual patterns are predictable.

❖ The eyes and the brain must work together to "think" about given information.

❖ Tolerance for ambiguity and perseverance are essential components for flexible, high-level visual thinking.

Materials

❖ One set of Combination Cards for EACH student, PLUS an additional set for the teacher (lamination recommended for use year after year)

❖ *Teacher Observation Checklist – Visual/Spatial Thinking*

Lesson Plan

1. Introduce the lesson by recalling the last whole class lesson activity in which students combined shapes together to make something new. You may even want to have a couple drawn out to help them recall the actual ones done in class together. Have students positioned so that it is difficult for them to look at each other's cards.

2. Begin by asking question #1: *Can you put the edges of the two cards together flat on the table in order to make a bow?*

3. Show any students who do not understand this how to do it, but do not give
    them credit for getting this one correct.

4. Continue with questions #2 - 5:

#1.   Can you put the edges of the two cards together
        flat on the table in order to make a bow?

        ****

#2.   Can you put the edges of the two cards together
        flat on the table in order to make a kite?

#3.   Can you put the edges of the two cards together
        flat on the table in order to make a king?

#4.   Can you put the edges of the two cards together
        flat on the table in order to make an Upper Case
        "A" ?

#5.   Can you put the edges of the two cards together
        flat on the table in order to make a house?

        ****

#6.   Can you put the edges of the two cards together
        flat on the table in order to make something new?

5. Review all answers for #2 - 5 from above. This serves two purposes: children who could not get some of the answers are now shown how to get them; and by recapping the ones that have already been done, children will create new combinations for the last question:

   Can you put the edges of the two cards together flat on the table in order to make something new?

6. During this activity, gather student data on the *Teacher Observation Checklist – Visual/Spatial Thinking* for each child.

ANSWERS TO QUESTIONS:

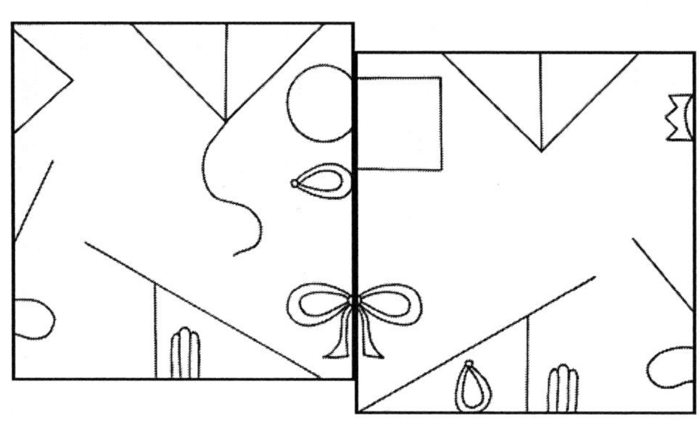

#1. Can you put the edges of the two cards together flat on the table in order to make a bow?

#2. Can you put the edges of the two cards together flat on the table in order to make a kite?

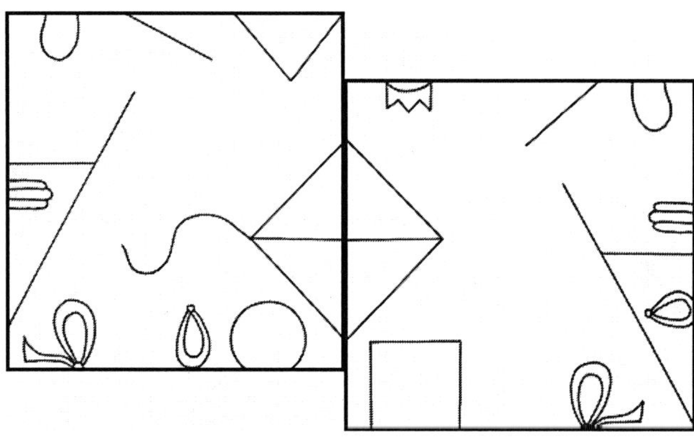

#3. Can you put the edges of the two cards together flat on the table in order to make a king?

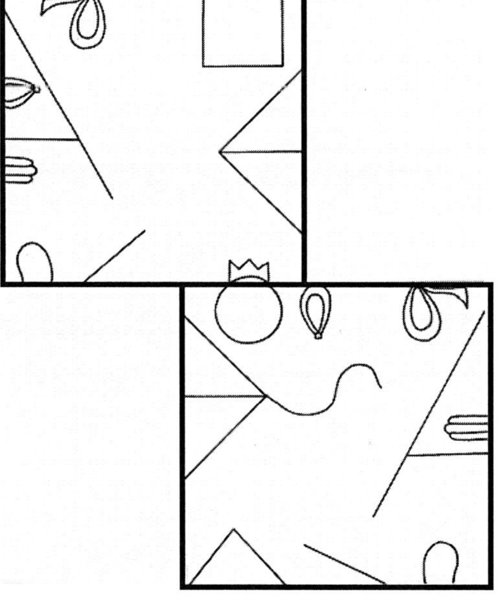

#4. Can you put the edges of the two cards together flat on the table in order to make an Upper Case "A?"

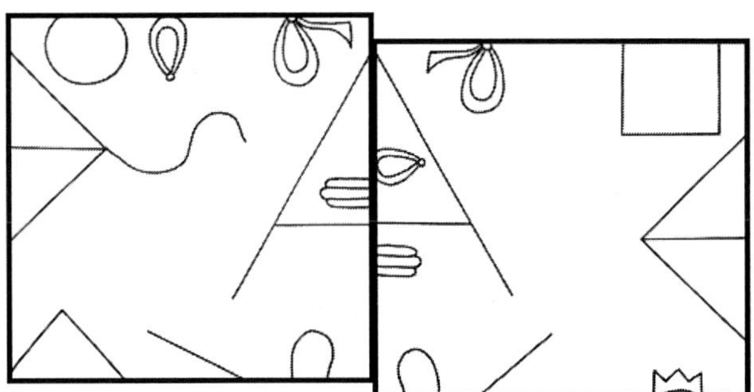

#5. Can you put the edges of the two cards together flat on the table in order to make a house?

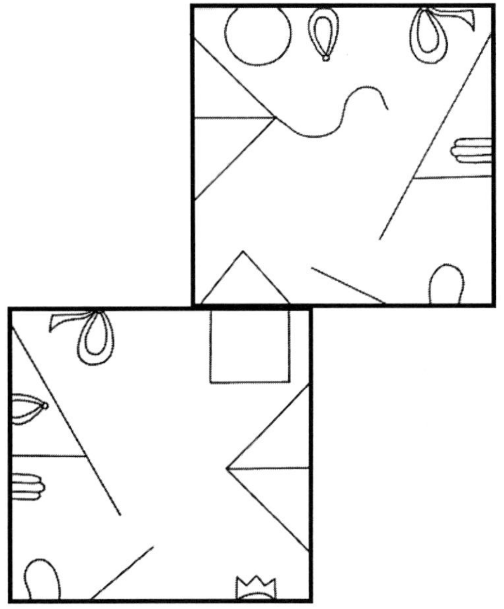

#6. Possible answers to the last question: hot dog in a bun, jellybean, a "V", etc.

Combination Cards

Resources & Extensions*
Visual/Spatial Thinking

<u>Analogies for Beginners</u> by Dianne Draze. (Prufrock Press, 1989)

- ❖ These analogies require students to analyze the elements of each puzzle, define relationships, and apply that relationship. Flexible and critical thinking are involved when completing the visual activities in this book.

<u>Disney's Mickey & Friends Activity Workbook</u> by Disney Enterprises, Inc. (Modern Publishing, 1998)

- ❖ These activity pages combine convergent and visual thinking by presenting visual outlines as clues in order to determine missing objects.

<u>The Dot Series</u> by Greta and Ted Rasmussen. (Tin Man Press, 2001)

- ❖ Who is Dot? Where is Dot? What is s/he doing? Use basic visual clues to answer these questions.

<u>First Time Analogies</u> by Dianne Draze. (Prufrock Press, 2005)

- ❖ These analogy activities are divided into four sections, each one presenting analogies with different formats and degrees of difficulty. Some of these lessons require visual analysis of relationships.

<u>The Hidden Alphabet</u> by Laura Seeger. (Roaring Brook Press, 2003)

- ❖ Examine the objects. Then lift the black frame to see what letter appears!

<u>I Spy: A Book of Picture Riddles</u> by Walter Wick & Jean Marzollo. (Scholastic, Inc., 1992)

- ❖ Picture riddles team up with visual discrimination to stimulate primary minds.

Look-Alikes by Joan Steiner. (Little, Brown and Co., 1998)

❖ With more than 1000 visual look-alikes to find, this book challenges both the mind and the eye.

Mystery Mansion by Michael Garland. (Dutton, 2001)

❖ As Tommy follows his aunt's clues to a mysterious surprise, he's surrounded by a visual feast of animals and letters – can you find them all?

Primarily Thinking by Judy Leimbach. (Prufrock Press, 2005)

❖ Activities that encourage finding visual patterns/relationships in order to think logically, identify relationships, make predictions, think flexibly, order sequences, and be persistent.

Seven Blind Mice by Ed Young. (Putnam Juvenile, 2002)

❖ For seven blind mice, wisdom comes from seeing the whole, not just the parts, of the strange Something in their midst.

Surprise in the Middle by Greta and Ted Rasmussen. (Tin Man Press, 2001)

❖ These activities combine convergent, divergent, and visual directions used as clues in order to create drawings. They encourage active listening and attention to visual details.

What Do You Do With a Tail Like This? by Steve Jenkins & Robin Page. (Houghton Mifflin, 2003)

❖ Can you identify the animal parts? To which animal does each belong and what does it do?

When a Line Bends … A Shape Begins by Rhonda Gowler Greene. (Houghton Mifflin, 1997)

❖ Explore many things that develop when a line becomes different shapes.

<u>You'll Never Guess!</u> by Fiona Dunbar. (Dial, 1991)

> ❖ A shape can become many things!

<u>Zoom</u> by Istvan Banyai. (Viking Press, 1995)

> ❖ In this exploration of visual perspective, nothing is as it seems.

*__Note:__ Too quickly, too often, really great books go unexpectedly out of print. Should you choose a resource that has suffered this sad fate, be sure to check out the second-hand booksellers at Amazon.com as many such titles may still be available through them.

Questions That Encourage
Visual/Spatial Thinking

Following is a generic set of questions designed to reinforce the visual/spatial thinking skills identified with each question. Use them with any extension resources. The questions are presented in three formats:

- In a list with specific thinking skills and some suggested applications filled in;

- On strips to copy and cut apart for flexibility of use – in random order or in a planned sequence; and

- On Q'ubes™ -- question cubes that students can toss and roll for a more active, kinesthetic involvement in the questioning process.

Encourage your students to pose their own questions for others in the class to answer. According to Socrates and John Dewey, a lot more thinking goes into such "active" questioning than into answering questions.

The Questions

What do you "see" when you think about this story?
- Mental imaging
- Relationships
- Abstraction

How would you describe ____________? What does he/she/it look like?
- Mental imaging
- Attributes

What do you like or dislike about the pictures in this book?
- Visual analysis
- Evaluative thinking, especially if reasons are given

Why do you think the illustrator drew the pictures this way?
- Visual analysis
- Inductive reasoning

How many details can you recall about ____________?
- Visual memory
- Attributes
- How many details can you recall about *[a character in the story]*?
- How many details can you recall about *[a place in the story]*?
- How many details can you recall about *[an object in the story]*?

What symbol would you use to stand for your favorite character?
- Mental imagining
- Relationships
- Attributes

What do you "see" when you think about this story?
What symbol would you use to stand for your favorite character?
How would you describe __________ ? What does he/she/it look like?
What do you like or dislike about the pictures in this book?
Why do you think the illustrator drew the pictures this way?
How many details can you recall about __________ ?

A PETS™ Q'UBE
Visual
Thinking

What do you "see" when you think about this story?

What symbol would you use to stand for your favorite character?

How would you describe ____________?
What does he/she/it look like?

What do you like or dislike about the pictures in this book?

Why do you think the illustrator drew the pictures this way?

How many details can you recall about ____________?

Stuff this cube with old plastic bags or styrofoam peanuts.

Then wrap with packing tape for durability.

OR

Enlarge cells to desired size.

Cut out and glue to the sides of a larger cardboard box.

<u>Notes</u>

Evaluative/Critical Thinking

During the whole class lesson, the teacher and observer are looking for students who are able to make choices and offer solutions that are based on factual, measurable, or observable considerations. These students recognize more than one viewpoint and understand how different considerations, or criteria, can affect outcome. They can support their decisions and opinions. Students who display much enthusiasm during the activities should be observed carefully as well.

Diagnostic Notes

An observation checklist is provided. Use the same checklist for both whole class and small group lessons. This way all of the data is together on one sheet. The following is a short summary of what to look for in student behaviors:

GRASPS CONCEPTS QUICKLY – Look for students who are able to understand quickly the concept of using factual, observable, or measurable considerations to eliminate choices and make a decision.

LOGICALLY SUPPORTS RESPONSES/OPINIONS -- Look for students who offer opinions based on factual, observable, or measurable considerations.

OFFERS UNUSUAL CONSIDERATIONS -- Look for students who provide considerations that have not been previously stated. These considerations may even surprise the teacher.

DRAWS VALID CONCLUSIONS BASED ON CONSIDERATIONS – These students can accurately apply valid considerations or criteria in order to help narrow the field of many choices regardless of their own personal preferences.

SEES MORE THAN ONE VIEWPOINT – Look for students who are able to see the issue from another's viewpoint. This also shows strong potential. Especially notable are any students who are able to develop their own valid, factual criterion from the other viewpoint.

Kindergarten PETS -- Teacher Observation Checklist
EVALUATIVE/CRITICAL THINKING

Teacher: ___________________ School Year: ___________________

Student Names	Grasps Concepts Quickly	Logically Supports Responses/Opinions	Offers Unusual Considerations	Draws Valid Conclusions Based on Considerations	Sees More Than One Viewpoint	Teacher Observations	TOTALS

Evaluative/Critical
Judge Thinking
Whole Class
Lesson 1

Purpose

The purpose of this lesson is to introduce students to criterion-based **Judge Thinking (evaluative/critical reasoning)** that bases decisions on factual, observable, or measurable considerations (or criteria) resulting from logical inquiry and reasoning. Criterion-based evaluative/critical thinking focuses on the following concepts:

❖ There is no one right answer.

❖ From amongst many possible choices, considerations (or criteria) can help guide students to the best choices.

❖ Decisions will be based on valid factual or observable considerations, not opinions.

❖ Students will be able to support/justify their choices.

Materials

❖ One copy of the book <u>Can I Have a Stegosaurus, Mom? Can I? Please!?</u> by Lois G. Grambling (classroom-sized books are best if available)

❖ Or one of these titles that follow the same premise:
   o <u>Can I Bring My Pterodactyl to School, Ms. Johnson?</u>
   o <u>I Wanna Iguana</u>
   o <u>Can I Have a Tyrannosaurus Rex, Dad? Can I? Please!?</u>

❖ *Teacher Observation Checklist – Evaluative/Critical Thinking*

Lesson Plan

1. Introduce the lesson by asking the students if they have ever asked their parents for something and were told "no." Explain how different "reasons" are considered when we are told "yes" or "no" and that they are called **considerations** (or **criteria**).

2. Tell the students that they are about to hear a story about a boy who comes up with all kinds of reasons why his mother should let him have a stegosaurus.

3. It is important that Kindergarteners continue to change venues, so at this point you may wish to ask them to move to a reading area in which to share the story. This way all students can clearly see the pictures.

4. During the activity below, the classroom teacher will gather data on the *Teacher Observation Checklist – Evaluative/Critical Thinking* provided with each student's name on it.

5. Begin to read <u>Can I Have a Stegosaurus? Can I? Please!?</u> by Lois G. Grambling. Read the story straight through making sure that each child gets to see each picture.

6. Once the book has been completed, ask the students to return to their desks or tables. At this point, ask, *"Who would like to come up and act out being a child asking his mother for a stegosaurus?"* Then ask another child to pretend to be the stegosaurus. The PETS™ teacher will be the mother. As a part of this role-playing, the "child" must present factual or observable "reasons" or considerations for his choice.

   What is unacceptable in this activity is a value judgment, such as, *"Because I like it"* or *"Because it's nice."* The "mother" will need to probe in such instances for the factual or observable element that makes this animal likeable or nice in this "child's" eyes by asking: *"Why do you think it's nice?"* or *"What is it that I can see that you like about this animal?"* The underlying considerations or criteria <u>must</u> be factual or observable.

   Should bribery come into the conversation (*"I'll keep my room clean if I can have a stegosaurus."*), the "mother" will need to redirect the conversation away from ways in which to acquire this pet back to reasons <u>why</u> it is the pet of choice.

   Continue until each child who wishes to participate gets to express him or herself by acting out at least one part.

This is also a perfect opportunity to remind students that as we learned while doing Inventor Thinking, we are just brainstorming considerations right now and <u>no</u> one's ideas are silly or should be laughed at.

7. At the end of this activity, the teacher may want to pretend to be the stegosaurus and go around the room on all fours acting like a dinosaur (occasionally even crawling up onto one of the classroom tables and sitting). This out-of-the-ordinary adult participation encourages children who might not normally take a risk to change their minds and feel freer about acting out one of the roles, too.

© Pieces of Learning

Evaluative/Critical
Judge Thinking
Whole Class
Lesson 2

Purpose

The purpose of this lesson is to reinforce criterion-based **Judge Thinking (evaluative/critical reasoning)** that bases decisions on factual, observable, or measurable considerations (or criteria) resulting from logical inquiry and reasoning. Criterion-based evaluative/critical thinking focuses on the following concepts:

❖ There is no one right answer.

❖ From amongst many possible choices, considerations (or criteria) can help guide students to the best choices.

❖ Decisions will be based on valid factual or observable considerations, not opinions.

❖ Students will be able to support/justify their choices.

Materials

❖ One copy of the book <u>The Little Mouse, the Red Ripe Strawberry, and the Big Hungry Bear</u> by Don and Audrey Wood (classroom-sized books are best if available).

❖ *Teacher Observation Checklist – Evaluative/Critical Thinking*

Lesson Plan

1. Introduce the lesson by asking the students how many of them like strawberries.

2. Tell the students that they will be hearing a story that is about a little mouse and a strawberry. All the little mouse wants is to eat that strawberry all by himself, but someone is playing a trick on him. To begin with, the students need to see if they can figure out who it is who is playing the trick.

3. It is important that Kindergarteners continue to change venues, so at this point you may wish to ask them to move to a reading area in which to share the story. This way all students can clearly see the pictures.

4. During the activity below, the classroom teacher will gather data on the *Teacher Observation Checklist – Evaluative/Critical Thinking* provided with each student's name on it.

5. Begin to read <u>The Little Mouse, the Red, Ripe Strawberry, and the Big Hungry Bear</u> by Don and Audrey Wood. Read the story straight through making sure each child gets to see each picture.

6. Once the book has been completed, ask the students to return to their desks or tables. At this point, ask if anyone knows who the big, hungry bear might really be.

    ❖ Does anyone know who the big, hungry bear is?
    ❖ Is there a big, hungry bear? Or is it the person reading the book?
    ❖ Why did you decide that? What were your considerations?

7. Should the little mouse have the strawberry all to himself? As a group, brainstorm a list of questions or considerations to determine if the little mouse should have the strawberry all to himself. Record these on chart paper for group discussion, for personal reflection, and for later small group use. Your list may include considerations such as:

    ❖ Can the little mouse eat ALL of that strawberry by himself?
    ❖ Do strawberries make a good diet for mice?
    ❖ Just how hungry is the little mouse?
    ❖ Might the strawberry spoil before the little mouse can finish it?

8. If the little mouse had decided to keep the whole strawberry …

    ❖ What other tricks to protect the strawberry might work even better than the ones the little mouse thought to use? Why do you think your idea is better?

This is another perfect opportunity for reminding students that as we learned while doing Inventor Thinking, we are just brainstorming right now -- <u>no</u> one's ideas are silly nor should we laugh at them.

          © Pieces of Learning

Evaluative/Critical
Judge Thinking
Small Group Lesson

Purpose

The purpose of this lesson is to apply criterion-based **Judge Thinking (evaluative/critical reasoning)** that bases decisions on factual, observable, or measurable considerations (or criteria) resulting from logical inquiry and reasoning. Remind students that:

- ❖ There is no one right answer.

- ❖ From amongst many possible choices, considerations (or criteria) can help guide them to the best choices.

- ❖ Decisions will be based on valid factual or observable considerations, not opinions.

- ❖ They will be able to support/justify their choices.

Materials

- ❖ List of responses/considerations from Evaluative/Critical Thinking – Whole Group Lesson 2

- ❖ A piece of large, 11"x17" white paper, pre-labeled with title and sentence starter for each student

- ❖ Crayons

- ❖ *Teacher Observation Checklist – Evaluative/Critical Thinking*

Lesson Plan

1. Prep illustration papers with title and sentence starter:

PETS
Evaluative

________________, can I please have a monster

because

2. Review with the students what factual and observable considerations or criteria
   are by using the list from Whole Group 2. Recall responses from Whole Group 1
   as well.

3. Explain that each student is to choose a monster for a pet and to determine an
   appropriate consideration in support of that choice.

4. The students will start by picking the person from whom the request will be made
   and writing that person's name on the line (e.g., "Mom" or "Dad") at the beginning
   of the sentence.

5. Students finish the sentences with individual considerations for choosing their
   monster as a pet. Be sure to <u>refocus</u> any value statements such as "because I
   like it" to a factual or observable consideration <u>for</u> liking it. Assist the non-writers
   with their sentences.

6. To complete this activity, the students draw individual pictures of their monsters
   that must reflect their personal considerations for their choices. See student
   sample on the next page.

Daddy, can I please have a monster because he can scare off strangers.

Resources & Extensions*
Evaluative Thinking

<u>Animals should definitely not wear clothing</u> by Judi Barrett. (Aladdin Paperbacks, 2001)

❖ Should animals wear clothing? Apparently not – as this book full of humorous considerations makes clear!

<u>Can I Bring My Pterodactyl to School, Ms. Johnson</u> by Lois G. Grambling. (Charlesbridge Publishing, 2006)

❖ Citing a most creative array of advantageous considerations, a young boy pleads his case for bringing this prize he won to school.

<u>Can I Have a Stegosaurus, Mom? Can I? Please!?</u> by Lois Grambling & H.B. Lewis. (Troll Communications, 1998)
<u>Can I Have a Tyrannosaurus Rex, Dad? Can I? Please!?</u> by Lois Grambling & Penny L.C. Hauffee. (Troll Communications, 2000)

❖ A boy brainstorms many creative considerations for keeping a stegosaurus/T-Rex as a pet.

<u>Charlie Cook's Favorite Book</u> by Julia Donaldson. (Dial Books for Young Readers, 2006)

❖ Charlie Cook is reading his favorite book about a pirate who finds a book about Goldilocks who is reading her favorite book about … where will it end? And why did each reader choose each book?

<u>Don't Let the Pigeon Drive the Bus</u> by Mo Willems. (Hyperion Books for Children, 2003)

❖ Are there positive as well as negative reasons for letting Pigeon drive the bus?

<u>Emma's Pet</u> by David McPhail. (Puffin Books, 1988)

❖ Emma considers different animal traits in choosing a new pet.

<u>I Call My Hand Gentle</u> by Amanda Haan. (Viking, 2003)

❖ Brainstorm all the things a hand can do, both positive and negative.

I Wanna Iguana by Karen Kaufman Orloff. (Scholastic Inc., 2004)

> ❖ Alex wants Mikey Gulligan's baby iguana for a pet and has to convince his mother that it's a good idea.

The Important Book by Margaret Wise Brown. (HarperTrophy, 1977)

> ❖ What's important about ordinary things.

My Lucky Day by Keiko Kasza. (Putnam, 2003)

> ❖ A pig accidentally enters the lair of a fox and must figure out the best way to keep from being eaten.

Primarily Thinking by Judy Leimbach. (Prufrock Press, 2005)

> ❖ Activities for distinguishing fact (proven & not open for dispute) from opinion (ideas that may differ from one person to another).

Things that are most in the world by Judi Barrett. (Aladdin Paperbacks, 2001)

> ❖ What is the wiggliest thing in the world? A snake ice-skating! What's the silliest … the quietest … the prickliest???

The Trial of Cardigan Jones by Tim Egan. (Houghton Mifflin, 2004)

> ❖ Cardigan Jones, a moose, is put on trial for stealing an apple pie. Did he do it? Let the readers be the jury!

William's Doll by Charlotte Zolotow. (HarperTrophy Books, 1985)

> ❖ William wants a doll – what needs to be considered?

***Note:** Too quickly, too often, really great books go unexpectedly out of print. Should you choose a resource that has suffered this sad fate, be sure to check out the second-hand booksellers at Amazon.com as many such titles may still be available through them.

Questions That Encourage
Evaluative/Critical Thinking

Following are two generic sets of questions designed to reinforce the evaluative/critical thinking skills identified with each question. Use them with any extension resources. The questions are presented in three formats:

- In a list with specific thinking skills and some suggested applications filled in;

- On strips to copy and cut apart for flexibility of use – in random order or in a planned sequence; and

- On Q'ubes™ -- question cubes that students call toss and roll for a more active, kinesthetic involvement in the questioning process.

There are two tiers of questions. The first Tier of questions includes those that are simpler and less open-ended than the questions in Tier 2 in order to allow you to differentiate for different readiness levels in your students.

Encourage your students to pose their own questions for others in the class to answer. According to Socrates and John Dewey, a lot more thinking goes into such "active" questioning than into answering questions.

The Questions
Tier 1

Did you enjoy this story? Why or why not?
- Making an analytical judgment
- Supporting judgment with considerations/criteria

What was the most important thing that happened in this story? Why?
- Rating by value
- Making an analytical judgment
- Supporting judgment with considerations/criteria

Who is the most important character in this story? Why do you think so?
- Rating by value
- Making an analytical judgment
- Justifying choice with considerations/criteria

If you could be any character in the story, who would you be? Why?
- Making an analytical choice
- Justifying choice with considerations/criteria

What did you like <u>best</u> about this story? Why?
- Prioritizing
- Making an analytical choice
- Justifying choice with considerations/criteria

How does this story make you feel? Why?
- Identifying reactions
- Justifying reactions with considerations/criteria

The Questions
Tier 2

Why do you think we read <u>this</u> story today?
- Drawing inferences
- Justifying perspective with considerations/criteria

Is this a great story? Give three reasons why or why not.
- Making an analytical judgment
- Supporting judgment with considerations/criteria
- Fluency of thought (divergent thinking)

Why is this story better and/or worse than ______________?
- Making an analytical judgment
- Supporting judgment with considerations/criteria
- Compare/contrast analysis
- Why is this story better and/or worse than *[name another story you've read with your students]*?

Do you think ___________ made the best decision? Why or why not?
- Making an analytical judgment
- Justifying position with considerations/criteria
- Do you think *[name a character in the story]* made the best decision? Why or why not?

What words did the author use that you really liked? Why?
- Making analytical choices
- Justifying choices with considerations/criteria

What kind of award do you think this book deserves? Why?
- Making an analytical judgment
- Justifying choice with considerations/criteria
- Originality (when a new sort of award is created)

© Pieces of Learning

Did you enjoy this story?
Why or why not?

What was the most important thing that happened in this story? Why?

Who is the most important character in this story? Why do you think so?

If you could be any character in the story, who would you be? Why?

What did you like <u>best</u> about this story? Why?

How does this story make you feel? Why?

Questions That Encourage Evaluative Thinking
Tier 2

Why do you think we read <u>this</u> story today?

Is this a great story? Give three reasons why or why not.

Why is this story better and/or worse than _____________ ?

Do you think _________ made the best decision? Why or why not?

What words did the author use that you really liked? Why?

What kind of award do you think this book deserves? Why?

A PETS™ Q'UBE
Evaluative
Thinking

Tier 1

Did you enjoy this story? Why or why not?

If you could be any character in the story, who would you be? Why?

Who is the most important character in this story? Why do you think so?

What was the most important thing that happened in this story? Why do you think so?

What did you like _best_ about this story? Why?

How does this story make you feel? Why?

Stuff this cube with old plastic bags or styrofoam peanuts.

Then wrap with packing tape for durability.

OR

Enlarge cells to desired size.

Cut out and glue to the sides of a larger cardboard box.

A PETS™ Q'UBE
Evaluative
Thinking

Tier 2

Why do you think we read <u>this</u> story today?

Is this a great story? Give three reasons why or why not.

Why is this story better and/or worse than ____________?

Do you think ____________ made the best decision? Why or why not?

What words did the author use that you really liked? Why?

What kind of award do you think this book deserves? Why?

Stuff this cube with old plastic bags or styrofoam peanuts.

Then wrap with packing tape for durability.

OR

Enlarge cells to desired size.

Cut out and glue to the sides of a larger cardboard box.

Notes

The PETS™ Higher Level Thinking Skills Series

By Jody Nichols, Sally Thomson, Margaret Wolfe, and Dodie Merritt

Thinking specialists Dudley the Detective, Isabel the Inventor, Sybil the Scientist, Max the Magician, Yolanda the Yarnspinner, and Jordan the Judge take primary students on an empowering problem-solving journey through divergent, convergent, evaluative, and visual thinking strategies in this ready-to-use, self-contained curriculum.

Both instructional and diagnostic, this curriculum exposes all your students to higher level thinking skills, provides challenging activities for talented learners, and builds behavioral portfolios that support identifying gifted students.

Each leveled book includes twenty-four detailed lesson plans of read-aloud/along stories, reproducible whole class activities and games, additional materials for enrichment and small group work, and behavioral assessments. Use these building blocks of thinking to establish a firm foundation for successful reading, writing, and learning in your students.

CLC0483 PETS™ 1 K-3rd

CLC0484 PETS™ 2   1st 3rd

CLC0503 PETS™ 3 1st – 4th

Staff Development with Co-Author Dodie Merritt

P.E.T.S.™ (Primary Education Thinking Skills) is a two-tier delivery system that is easily facilitated by the classroom teacher or a visiting specialist. Participants in Dodie's workshop will learn the P.E.T.S.™ curriculum progression so they can use it in their classrooms, discover behaviors to identify that indicate potential high-level thinkers, and discover activities that help identify and then encourage high-level thinking in primary children. Thinking skills include convergent, deductive, divergent, visual, and evaluative thinking. P.E.T.S.™ is also diagnostic. The behavioral checklist used during whole group activities helps identify high-level thinkers for small group instruction. P.E.T.S.™ originated in the Crystal Lake, Illinois, school district and has been adopted by other primary classroom teachers throughout the United States. Call Pieces of Learning at 1-800-729-5137 to schedule Dodie for dynamic, practical staff development.

